Advance Praise for *Getting Back to Happy*

"A powerful and easy-to-read tour of what it means to be a human being. Marc and Angel shine a personally and psychologically practical light on the surprising ways in which we distract ourselves from what matters most in life, through good times and bad. *Getting Back to Happy* is a must-read guide for getting back on track."

—Lewis Howes, *New York Times* bestselling author of
The School of Greatness and *The Mask of Masculinity*

"If you are skeptical of those who say they can help you transform a painful, troubled life into one of fulfillment and peace, you need to know Angel and Marc Chernoff. *Getting Back to Happy* feels like an enlightening heart-to-heart conversation with wise and loving mentors. Through inspiring anecdotes and practical strategies, Angel and Marc lay out the step-by-step revolutionary process that allowed them to move from despair and desolation to hope and positivity. *Getting Back to Happy* is much more than one couple's journey from rock bottom; it is a familiar hand in the darkness, leading you to the light of possibility and hope that's been within you all along."

—Rachel Macy Stafford, *New York Times* bestselling author of
Hands Free Mama, Hands Free Life and *Only Love Today*

"*Getting Back to Happy* is a must-read for complex times. You can't control everything that happens to you in this crazy world, but you can control your response to it. Marc and Angel provide a grace-filled guide to navigate life and find happiness regardless of your circumstances."

—Joshua Becker, founder of Becoming Minimalist
and author of *The More of Less*

"I'm a big fan of advice based on real experience and wisdom that reconnects us to some deeper sense of self and helps awaken a sense of potential. I also appreciate genuine insights that inspire shifts in perspective and attitude about what is and is not possible. *Getting Back to Happy* has all of this and more!"

—Jonathan Fields, founder of Good Life Project
and author of *How to Live a Good Life*

"*Getting Back to Happy* invites us to change our lives by changing our thoughts. The powerful lessons and action steps delivered throughout the book, mixed with beautiful stories of people experiencing heartbreak, trauma, and hopelessness who rise up, don't just bring us back to happy—they bring us back to hope, to love, and to trusting ourselves to live rich lives full of what matters most.

—Courtney Carver, author of *Soulful Simplicity*

"Marc and Angel have written an easy-to-follow, wonderfully empowering guide to help you cultivate a deep and pervasive sense of well-being and happiness. Their down-to-earth, practical advice will provide you with a strong, solid inner foundation for life's ups and downs, and support you to be resourceful in the face of any challenges you may face along the way."

—Katherine Woodward Thomas, *New York Times bestselling* author of *Calling in "The One"* and *Conscious Uncoupling*

"*Getting Back to Happy* is a powerful collection of candid, at times raw, life lessons accompanied by the perfect balance of professional research and specific techniques that will undoubtedly lay the foundation for drastic, positive changes across nearly every aspect of our lives."

—Dr. Kristin M. Tolbert, PsyD, licensed psychologist

"As a martial arts and fitness trainer, athlete, husband, father, business owner, and entrepreneur, *Getting Back to Happy* was a lifesaver to me in countless ways. Filled with actionable insights and strategies for important skills like building healthy daily rituals, staying mindful while under stress, working through impossible situations, and finding silver linings of happiness through it all, the book not only improved my life, but also equipped me with healthy ideas to pass on to my students and athletes."

—John Hackleman, trainer of UFC champions

tarcherperigee

An imprint of Penguin Random House LLC
375 Hudson Street
New York, New York 10014

Most TarcherPerigee books are available at special quantity discounts for bulk purchase for sales promotions, premiums, fund-raising, and educational needs. Special books or book excerpts also can be created to fit specific needs. For details, write: SpecialMarkets@ penguinrandomhouse.com.

LIBRARY OF CONGRESS CATALOGING-IN-PUBLICATION DATA

Names: Chernoff, Marc, author. | Chernoff, Angel, author.
Title: Getting back to happy: change your thoughts, change your reality, and turn your trials into triumphs / Marc & Angel Chernoff.
Description: New York : TarcherPerigee, [2018]
Identifiers: LCCN 2017058110 (print) | LCCN 2017059401 (ebook) | ISBN 9780525504665 | ISBN 9780143132776
Subjects: LCSH: Change (Psychology) | Attitude (Psychology) | Happiness.
Classification: LCC BF637.C4 (ebook) | LCC BF637.C4 C46 2018 (print) | DDC 158.1—dc23
LC record available at https://lccn.loc.gov/2017058110

Printed in the United States of America
1   3   5   7   9   10   8   6   4   2

Book design by Elke Sigal

GETTING BACK TO HAPPY

Change Your Thoughts, Change Your Reality,
and Turn Your Trials into Triumphs

MARC & ANGEL CHERNOFF

A TarcherPerigee Book

GETTING
BACK TO
HAPPY

Contents

Foreword

We're all on a journey to become who we truly are—our strongest, bravest, truest selves. This journey isn't always a smooth or easy one. Many of us have years, or even decades, of "lessons" to unlearn—about accepting less than we deserve, being "good" instead of speaking up, seeing ourselves as less than, simply because people have treated us that way for so long.

In my own journey to uncover who I truly am, and to find—and use—my voice for what I believe in, I've been lucky enough to meet many kindred spirits along the way, many of them online. Marc and Angel are among the fellow travelers I've come to value the most. Their honesty and clarity, and the generous way they share what they've learned, are gifts I've truly cherished. Sharing their ideas with others online is a way of paying forward what I've learned, in the hope that others will gain some insight and strength, and in turn spread the word even further. The pain of self-doubt and the isolation of modern life can make us feel like we're the only ones struggling, while everyone else is picture-perfect. That's why it's so important to share not just our triumphs but also our setbacks, to "show our work" when we're in the thick of tough times. Marc and Angel do just that—keeping it real, and creating a community of kindred spirits that gathers together in strength, growing and learning along the way.

Life is always going to throw us curveballs—surprises and setbacks we didn't see coming. Jaw-dropping, momentum-crushing moments that make you question everything you've worked so hard to achieve, as well as flat gray days when the light just won't shine in. But there's *always* a way forward. With the help of Marc and Angel's hard-won insights, we can always find a way to pick ourselves up, reframe our mindset to see the bigger picture, and take that first step back to happy. It isn't always easy, and you might ruffle some feathers among those who aren't used to seeing you stand up for yourself. But the inner strength to move forward toward truth and light is a muscle each one of us has. Use it. Own it. And help others do the same. We're all in this together—but we have to take that first step on our own. Pass it on.

Alyssa Milano

Introduction

You have to do hard things to be happy in life. The things most people avoid, such as those that make you uncomfortable, that are far easier to hide from, that others can't do for you, that make you second-guess yourself and question how you're going to find the strength to push forward.

Why?

Because the hard things ultimately build you up and change your life. They make the difference between existing and living, between knowing the path and walking it, between a lifetime of empty promises and one filled with progress and fulfillment.

We know this now, but we didn't until we hit rock bottom.

At the lowest point in our lives—when we were stuck in a shared bout of depression and every step forward was difficult to even consider—we learned the hard things were in fact the right things. They provided the only logical path forward.

A Difficult Conversation, and Why

We had just lost two loved ones to death, then we lost our family's primary source of income. It all happened suddenly and in quick succession. Our lives came to a halt, for months, as we desperately struggled to cope with our new reality.

As Marc recalls it:

"On your deathbed, it's too late to honor and respect the people you've lost," Angel said.

I kept a downward gaze, but nodded my head in agreement.

Through her tears, she continued. "On your deathbed, it's too late to truly prove your love to the people you love."

Again I solemnly nodded, but this time I felt inspired to add, "On your deathbed, it's too late to pick flowers for your wife."

Angel quickly glanced at the flowers sitting on our nightstand, cracked a half smile, scooted across our bed, and rested her head on my shoulder.

I continued. "On your deathbed, it's too late to be who you might have been. To make wish lists, to do the hard things required to check them off, and to appreciate the little bits of daily progress you're making on your journey back to happy."

. . .

That's a taste of a conversation we had on a Friday ten years ago at three o'clock in the morning.

We were both up because we couldn't sleep.

We couldn't sleep because we had just lost loved ones back-to-back to illness and suicide.

We couldn't sleep because without a new source of income in a brutal economic recession, we feared we'd be on the streets soon.

We didn't know how to sleep and cry at the same time.

Yet somehow, in the dark, we found hope in a really difficult and slightly twisted conversation about our deathbeds and the obvious fact that neither of us was on ours yet.

Unbeknownst to us, that conversation was the beginning of our journey back to happy.

But let me back up for a moment and tell you how we got to that conversation in the middle of the night.

It was five o'clock in the morning in San Diego the day after my twenty-seventh birthday. Angel and I had been up late the night before celebrating at a local sports bar with some friends. And we would have slept in for a few more hours if both of our phones hadn't started ringing nonstop.

"Who in their right mind is calling us this early?" Angel muttered as she rolled out of bed.

"I don't know. Just turn the ringers off and come back to bed," I said as she walked into the living room to check our phones.

But as soon as Angel glanced at the phones she knew something was wrong. There were more than a dozen missed calls and text messages from some of our closest friends and family on the East Coast. One of the text messages read "Have you heard about Josh?" She called for me to take a look. And that turned out to be the very last moment we still had hope we'd share another good laugh with one of the kindest human beings we've ever known— one of our very best friends.

Josh died from cardiac arrest (provoked by an asthma attack) in the middle of the night at the age of twenty-seven, leaving behind his wife, Cami (who now works with us), and their two baby boys, Ethan and Jacob.

A few weeks after Josh passed away, Angel's older brother, Todd, died by suicide—he was only thirty-six, and had a constant smile that made everyone around him smile too. Why did he do it? Why didn't we know he had lost hope behind his contagious smile? Those questions haunted us in every waking moment for a long,

long time. We cried a lot. For him. For Josh. For both of them at once.

And as our hearts and minds hit rock bottom, so too did the economy.

Angel had lost her breadwinning job during our struggles with loss, in one of the worst job markets in U.S. history. So with two broken hearts, we were forced to reinvent ourselves not only on a personal level, but on a professional one too. And it certainly didn't happen overnight. We had a lot to learn before we'd be back on our feet again.

Getting Back to Happy: The Book

Although our journey has been anything but easy, we're whole-heartedly grateful for the lessons we gleaned as we battled our way through it, one day at a time. These life lessons are the basis for our blog, for our life work teaching others from our experience, and now for this book. The key to our progress and evolution has been building specific daily rituals that gradually allowed us to do the hard things no one else could do for us, to heal, to grow, and to move our lives forward again—which is precisely what this book will show you how to do.

Based on our personal journey, extensive positive psychology research, and over a decade's worth of life coaching with hundreds of coaching clients, course students, and live-event attendees, this book will guide you through a daily process of learning how to change your thinking and behavior so you can turn major and minor trials into personal triumphs. During the process that ulti-mately led to the creation of this book, we asked ourselves hard questions such as:

- Where can we discover the silver linings of the issues we're dealing with?
- Where are the opportunities for growth, understanding, and learning in the midst of our present struggles?
- Are the stories echoing repeatedly in our heads really true?
- How are we defined by these stories?
- If we were able to let go of these stories—to grow beyond ourselves and change our perspective—what else might we experience, and what about these stories would no longer seem true?

When we took the time to answer these questions thoughtfully and honestly, sometimes we were surprised by what we learned about ourselves. Ultimately we discovered new ways of thinking and looking at our circumstances that totally transformed our lives.

Since then, we've dedicated our efforts to teaching others that working with their stories can help them overcome whatever darkness they're facing. In 2006, we started our blog, *Marc & Angel Hack Life* (www.marcandangel.com), as a passion project—a place to hold ourselves accountable to a positive, healthy, and mindful shift in our thinking. It gave us a platform, not just as a personal account-ability journal for each other, but as a shared experience with others who were—and continue to be—on the same journey. We find this work to be deeply rewarding and inspiring, and we feel so fortunate to have the opportunity to help others.

Marc & Angel Hack Life, now with two million page views each month, is a place people go for guidance on thinking and living better—mentally, emotionally, spiritually, and physically. As the blog has grown over the years, we've expanded the reach and depth of our message through one-on-one and small group coaching sessions. We also hold live conferences, one of which is titled "Think Better, Live Better" (thinklivebetter.com), and we speak at national conferences and events. In each of these settings, we encounter courageous souls who are searching for the means within themselves that will enable them to climb out of the darkness.

We do an exercise in our live events where we tell people to look around the room and find the color red. So they look carefully and start to see red everywhere. After a minute or two, we say, "Now close your eyes, and think about every place in the room you remember the color green." Everyone laughs, because they don't remember any green—they were looking for red. Even though green and red exist in the room at the same time, they don't see the green in their minds because their focus wasn't there.

We help people see the green—the whole picture—in their present lives.

We help people like Michelle, one of hundreds of amazing students who took our online course, also titled "Getting Back to Happy." When she signed up for the course, Michelle was in a dark place. After taking some time off to help one of her daughters with dyslexia and autism get into college and get settled, she was ready to reenter the workforce. For the first time in her life, she found herself struggling to find work. She would get to the final round of interviews and be turned down. This kept happening for more than a year and a half, and Michelle felt deeply discouraged and broken.

Hard times had hit, and not just financially. Her brother had died by suicide. Her mother had fallen and broken her hip and now needed in-home care. Her home had flooded, causing massive damage and expensive repairs. And her marriage of thirty years was falling apart due to a lack of connection and intimacy and a partner with an alcohol addiction. Her feelings of being stuck and lost got so bad she remembers one Christmas when her friends had to come over and get her out of bed because she was lying in the dark, unable to get up and face the world anymore.

"I had all 'the things,'" Michelle says. "But it just didn't mean anything anymore. I was in a toxic marriage. I didn't want my kids to experience a divorce, and I kept trying to hold on. I was looking for a job and going from one rejection to the next. I couldn't seem to make anything happen. It was depressing, and I was losing hope. I knew I needed to make some changes."

Michelle couldn't dig herself out of the rut she was in, at least not alone, but hope and change were coming. After working through the course and completing the included one-on-one coaching calls with us, Michelle finally understood how she was unconsciously following patterns that were holding her back. When she began breaking those patterns, she started to find the peace of mind, clarity, and confidence she needed to make changes in her life. She learned that her journey was separate from her husband's; she learned practical ways to rebuild her self-esteem; and she learned how to accept life the way it is, not the way she wanted it to be.

Within a few months, Michelle found herself back in the workforce and rebuilding her life. Distancing herself from unhealthy relationships and getting back to work was just the beginning for Michelle and her children. She also started repairing damaged relationships with certain family members, enrolled her children in positive community programs, and began recovering financially and repairing her home. She learned how to make real progress as a single mother, as she had separated from her husband and supported his entering a long-term rehabilitation hospital. She gradually began living more joyfully in all areas of her life, no matter what was happening around her.

"Marc and Angel helped me learn how to let go," Michelle says. "They helped me think better no matter what was happening around me and return to being an energetic person ready to take on some of the hardest and most rewarding challenges of my life."

We love stories like Michelle's, and we have hundreds more like hers. Our goal for this book is to help you too learn how to think differently about the inevitable struggles you face, and provide you with the tools and strategies to cultivate a fresh perspective and make powerful positive changes. For every thought, there are many perspectives. If we can recognize the thought we're experiencing in the moment, we can train ourselves to focus on the angle that most benefits us, and then act accordingly. *Getting Back to Happy* is about seeing more than the rabbit hole of negative thinking we so often fall into. It is about controlling our thoughts and broadening our focus so we can make room for growth, opportunity, and healing.

> **If we can learn to think better, we can ultimately live better.**

When we're able to think more rationally about our present situation and expand our perspective, we're able to see the whole picture, beyond the narrow focus brought on by pain and disappointment. In other words, if we can learn to think better, we can ultimately live better. And we can then apply that principle to everything we do going forward. Learning to cultivate the big-picture perspective—considering the whole truth—isn't easy, but it eventually allows us to step forward and live better, no matter what happens next.

Let us quickly share three more stories with you . . .

- "On my nursing shift at the hospital this evening, I was forced into a moment of clarity when I got off my phone, utterly flustered after having an argument with my husband, and an eight-year-old patient who's dying of leukemia asked me if I was okay."
- "Today is the ten-year anniversary of the day I had planned on ending my life. It's also the ten-year anniversary of the day I found out I was pregnant with my now nine-year-old son. He's the reason I changed my mind. And he is so worth it! But perhaps most important, I now realize I am worth it too."
- "This afternoon I learned that the lady who I thought was a very young mom of the two twin girls I have in my fifth-grade math class is actually their twenty-five-year-old half sister, who is raising them after a tragic car accident took their parents."

These anecdotes have been transcribed with permission from coaching sessions we've recently conducted. And if there's one thing these students' stories have in common, it's the importance of our perspective. What we see in life—how we feel about ourselves, our lives, and the people around us—greatly depends on how we think. And the somewhat scary truth is, our perspective on just about everything comes from the psychological cage we've been conditioned to live in. A cage created by . . .

- A difficult or disappointing past
- A privileged or sheltered life
- Social influence
- Pop-culture and mass-media stereotyping

And the list goes on.

Gradually, unbeknownst to us, our cage—our conditioning—drains our mental energy, leaving us vulnerable to bad decision making. The key? There are many. And we're going to cover them extensively throughout this book. But in a nutshell, you have to learn to . . .

Doubt your doubts before you doubt your faith.

That's the supershort version of our advice for those moments when nothing seems to be going as planned; when everything you want seems out of reach; when you feel utterly stuck.

Yes, just be right where you are, with an open mind.

Let go of what you think your life is supposed to look like and sincerely appreciate it for everything it is.

Easier said than done, of course, especially when tragedy strikes. And although Angel and I have coped and grown through our fair share of real tragedies, which you will hear more about throughout this book, let's be honest about something: 98 percent of the time we create tragedy in our lives out of fairly minor incidents. Something doesn't go exactly as planned, but rather than learn from the experience, we freak out about it and let stress define us.

Our challenge for you is to start choosing differently—don't let the little things that are out of your control dominate you!

The biggest difference between peace and stress is attitude. It's all about how you look at a situation and what you decide to do with it. It's remembering that there are no certainties in life; we don't know exactly what the future will bring. So your best strategy for living is to make the best and most positive use of the present moment, even when it disappoints you . . .

Especially when it disappoints you!

How disappointed would you be to get twenty years down the road and discover you were meant to appreciate and enjoy life, while all you did was resist and doubt it?

Your life, with all its ups and downs, unexpected twists and turns, has brought you to this moment. It took each and every intricate, confusing, and painful situation you have encountered to bring you to right here, right now.

And if you have the courage to admit that you're a little scared, and have the ability to smile even as you cry, the nerve to ask for help when you need it, and the wisdom to take it when it's offered, then you have everything you need.

You just have to believe it so you can take the next step.

It's interesting how we all outgrow what we once thought we couldn't live without, and then we fall in love with what we didn't even know we wanted. This is part of living and growing as a human being. We discover more about who we are and the way life really is, and then we realize there are some changes we need to make. The lifestyle we've been living no longer fits. The environments and relationships we once found comfort in no longer exist, or no longer serve our best interests. So we cherish all the great memories, but find ourselves at a crossroads, choosing to embark on the first step of a brand-new path.

And it's not easy. It's painful to give up what's comfortable and familiar, especially when you have no other choice. Angel and I have struggled through this process many times out of necessity.

Over the past decade we've had to deal with several significant, un-expected life changes and challenges, including:

- Losing a sibling to suicide
- Losing a best friend to cardiac arrest
- Financial unrest and debt following a breadwinning employment layoff
- Breaking ties with a loved one who repeatedly betrayed us
- Family business failure (and reinvention)

Those experiences were brutal. Each of them knocked us down and off course for a while. But once we accepted the truth, by letting go of the way things used to be, we pressed forward, stronger and with a greater understanding of and respect for life.

Getting to the right state of mind, one that actually allowed us to move forward with our lives, required mindful practice. Because when we were initially faced with each one of those brutal experiences, you better believe our minds were spinning with negative emotions. We had to learn to catch ourselves in that negative state of emotional unrest, and then consciously calm our minds so we could think straight and make the best decisions possible.

In other words, we had to learn how to cope more effectively from the inside out so we could let go of the thoughts that were holding us back.

We met at the University of Central Florida when we were freshmen, and this is something our undergrad psychology professor alluded to cleverly, long before we fully grasped the importance of her wisdom. On the last day of class before graduation, she walked up on stage to teach one final lesson, which she called "a vital lesson on the power of perspective and mindset." As she raised a glass of water over her head, everyone expected her to mention the typical "glass half empty or glass half full" metaphor. Instead, with a smile on her face, our professor asked, "How heavy is this glass of water I'm holding?"

Students shouted out answers ranging from a couple of ounces to a couple of pounds.

After a few moments of fielding answers and nodding her head, she replied, "From my perspective, the absolute weight of this glass is irrelevant. It all depends on how long I hold it. If I hold it for a minute or two, it's fairly light. If I hold it for an hour straight, its weight might make my arm ache. If I hold it for a day straight, my arm will likely cramp up and feel completely numb and paralyzed, forcing me to drop the glass to the floor. In each case, the absolute weight of the glass doesn't change, but the longer I hold it, the heavier it feels to me."

As most of us students nodded our heads in agreement, she continued. "Your worries, frustrations, disappointments, and stressful thoughts are very much like this glass of water. Think about them for a little while and nothing drastic happens. Think about them a bit longer and you begin to feel noticeable pain. Think about them all day long, and you will feel completely numb and paralyzed, incapable of doing anything else until you drop them."

Think about how this relates to your life.

If you've been struggling to cope with the weight of what's on your mind, it's a strong sign that it's time to put the glass down.

The key is to realize that the vast majority of the worries, frustrations, disappointments, and stressful thoughts you're dealing with are a product of your own creation. And you can let them go quickly by learning how to cope more effectively with what you're feeling inside. How you deal with unexpected stress and frustration easily can be the difference between living a good life and living a troubled one. If you choose unhealthy coping mechanisms like avoidance or denial, for example, you can quickly turn a tough situation into a tragic one. And sadly, this is a common mistake many people make. When you find yourself facing a disheartening reality, your first reaction might be to deny the situation, or to avoid dealing with it altogether. But by doing so you're inadvertently holding on even tighter to the pain that you wish to let go of; in effect, you're sealing it up inside you.

Let's imagine someone close to you has become ill, and supporting this person through his or her illness is incredibly painful. You might not want to deal with the pain, so you cope by avoiding it, by finding ways to numb yourself with alcohol and unhealthy eating. And consequently, you become physically ill too while the pain continues to fester inside you.

Obviously, that's not good.

If you notice yourself doing something similar, it's time to pause, admit to yourself that you're coping by avoiding, and then shift your focus to a healthier coping mechanism by using the proven tools and strategies discussed throughout this book. These tools and strategies will open your mind when you need it most. Because when you face struggles with an attitude of openness— open to the painful feelings and emotions you have—you find out that it's not comfortable, but you can still be fine and you can still step forward. Openness means you don't instantly decide that you know this is going to be a horrible experience; it means you admit you don't really know what the next step will be like, and you'd like to understand the whole truth of the matter. It's a stance of learning instead of one that assumes the worst.

Coping certainly isn't an easy practice. But it's worth your while. With practice, healthy coping allows us to find better ways of managing life's continuous stream of unexpected and uncontrollable circumstances—from minor setbacks and challenges to life-changing loss. Instead of denying, avoiding, self-medicating, lashing out, and other common but unhealthy coping strategies, you'll discover healthier ways to meet whatever life throws your way, and come out stronger, and often even more fulfilled, than you were before. In the end, the world is as you are inside. What you think, you see and you ultimately become. And this book is your guide. Let's begin.

> What you think, you see and you ultimately become.

CHAPTER 1

Rituals: Practice Daily What You Want to Manifest Regularly

Carve out a little time every day to focus on the things that matter most, and the benefits will return to you exponentially.

"Today, on my forty-seventh birthday, I reread the suicide note I wrote on my twenty-seventh birthday about two minutes before my girl-friend, Carol, showed up at my apartment and told me she was pregnant. Her words were honestly the only reason I didn't follow through with it. Suddenly I felt I had something to live for, and I started making small positive changes one day at a time. It's been a journey, but Carol is now my wife and we've been happily married for nineteen years. And my daughter, who is now a twenty-one-year-old university student pursuing a degree in medicine, has two younger brothers. I read my suicide note every year on the morning of my birthday as a reminder to be grateful—I am grateful I stopped waiting and started doing things daily that ultimately gave me a second chance at life."

That's the opening paragraph of an email we received recently from a course student named Kevin. His words remind us that sometimes we have to endure our very darkest moments in order to be reborn and rise again as a stronger, happier version of our-selves. Although circumstances and people will occasionally break you down to the lowest of lows, when you keep your mind focused on the positive, your heart open to love, and continue to put one foot in front of the other, you can recover the pieces, rebuild, and come back much stronger and happier than you ever would have been otherwise.

Life is painful. Change is painful. Growth is painful. But in the end, nothing is as painful as staying stuck where you do not belong. It's always better to be exhausted from meaningful effort on a daily basis than to be tired of doing nothing. Too often we spend our days—and our lives—thinking about taking the important steps we never take. We suffer far longer than we have to simply because we don't step through the tragedies and challenges we face on a daily basis. And that's precisely why we're starting here, with a deep dive into the power of daily rituals. Let's press forward with another per-tinent story . . .

In 1911, two explorers, Roald Amundsen and Robert Falcon Scott, embarked on a race against each other to become the first known human being to set foot upon the southernmost point of Earth. It was the age of Antarctic exploration, as the South Pole represented one of the last uncharted areas in the world. Amundsen wished to plant the Norwegian flag there on behalf of his country, while Scott hoped to stake his claim for England.

The journey there and back from their base camps was about fourteen hundred miles, which is roughly equivalent to a round-trip hike from New York City to Chicago. Both men would be traveling the same distance on foot through extremely cold and harsh weather conditions. And both men were equally equipped with experience, supplies, and a supporting team of fellow explorers.

As it turned out, Amundsen and Scott took entirely different approaches to the very same challenges.

Scott directed his team to hike as far as possible on the good weather days and then rest on the bad weather days to conserve energy. Conversely, Amundsen directed his team to follow a strict regimen of consistent daily progress by hiking exactly twenty miles every day, regardless of weather conditions. Even on the warmest clear-sky days, when Amundsen's team was capable of hiking much farther, he was absolutely adamant that they travel no more than twenty miles to conserve their energy for the following day's hike.

Which team succeeded in the end?

Amundsen's team, the one that took consistent daily action.

Why?

Because what we do *every* day defines us.

Today's progress is always compounded by yesterday's effort, no matter how small.

And it all comes down to the power of self-discipline, which we discuss in detail soon. But for now, think about the most common problems we deal with in our modern lives, from lack of presence to lack of exercise to unhealthy diets to procrastination, and so forth. In most cases, problems like these are caused not by a physically present limitation, but by a limitation of the mind—specifically, a lack of self-discipline.

We put the hard things off until tomorrow for a variety of reasons, until we've lost our momentum. We grow accustomed to the belief that things should be easier than they are, and that waiting another day or two makes the most sense. Then one day we wake up and we're emotionally incapable of doing the hard things that need to be done.

Let this be your wake-up call!

Your mind and body both need to be exercised to gain strength. They need to be challenged, and they need to be worked consistently, to grow and develop over time. If you haven't pushed yourself in lots of little ways over time—if you always avoid doing the hard things—of course you'll crumble on the inevitable days that are harder than you expected.

And if we had to guess, we'd say Scott's team suffered in exactly this way. They tried to make things easier on themselves; the fantasy of "easier" became their mantra, their subconscious goal. But this fantasy was never going to be a reality during a fourteen-hundred-mile footrace to the South Pole.

Scott's team lost the race, not only on the ground, but in their minds first.

Don't follow in their footsteps!

No matter where you stand now, the next best step forward is yours for the taking. Will it be easy? Not likely. As you move forward in life, adversity is inescapable. Once you come out of the storm, you see yourself as you really are in raw form, without the baggage that's been holding you back. And that makes all the difference, because it frees you to take the next step, and the next.

We first learned this lesson a decade ago, shortly after we lost two loved ones to illness, lost our livelihood in a layoff, and ultimately lost sight of the goodness that remained in our lives. Like it was yesterday, we still vividly remember that rainy summer evening when Marc found himself lying on a cold floor, alone in the dark again, just thinking. Marc recalls that night:

Angel and I rarely spoke openly about anything meaningful during that period, mostly because I was withdrawn. I felt helpless and depressed about what had happened. I was lost in the darkness of my own negative thinking.

But something slightly shifted inside me as I was lying on that cold floor.

As I looked up and out the open window next to me, the moon suddenly broke through the clouds and illuminated the dark room I was in. Then, within seconds, a light breeze started blowing the white window curtains inward and over me. As the curtains fluttered four feet over my body, I smiled, for the first time in days. It was a beautiful moment. And without thinking twice, I whispered out loud, "Life is still a miracle to be grateful for."

Angel walked into the room at that exact moment and whispered, "I agree."

She ducked under the curtains and snuggled into me on the floor. After a couple moments of shared silence, we decided to list some things off the top of our heads that we were grateful for, despite our struggles:

- *We had each other.*
- *We had parents, extended family, and friends who loved us.*
- *We were reasonably healthy.*
- *Most of our family members and friends were reasonably healthy.*
- *We had some savings.*
- *We had shelter, water, and food.*
- *We could experience and appreciate the beauty of the moonlight illuminating the dark room we were in and the breeze making the curtains dance.*

And the list went on, of course, but you get the gist. Even when everything seemed to be wrong, we had a lot going right—a lot to be grateful for. That night I resolved to change my thinking and make gratitude a daily ritual in my life. I started spending fifteen minutes every evening focusing my thoughts exclusively on what I was grateful for and why. I called it my gratitude meditation. This may seem like a trivial, clichéd practice to some people, but a ritual like this changes lives.

Here's what has gradually changed in my life as I've practiced my ritual of gratitude:

- *I appreciate Angel more, and tell her so, which has ultimately deepened our relationship by opening us to more vulnerable and honest communication.*
- *I appreciate my extended family and close friends more, because I pay closer attention to their positive qualities.*
- *I have grown kinder to everyone around me, and kinder to myself too, because I have replaced many of my old, needless judgments with simple appreciation.*
- *Little frustrations bother me less, because I complain less.*
- *I need less to be happy, because I am being present and sincerely appreciating what I already have.*
- *I notice life's simple pleasures and little moments more than I ever have before.*
- *Working through life's inevitable difficulties has grown easier, because instead of focusing on how painful everything is, I find gratitude and joy in the small steps of progress I make every day.*

And this list goes on and on too. But the important thing to realize is that all of these changes are incredibly positive and powerful.

They aren't trivial, and they're far from being a cliché. My gratitude ritual has fundamentally changed the way I think and live.

Have no doubt: a simple ten-minute ritual can change your entire life. We began practicing a gratitude ritual because that was what we needed at the time. But whether it's to help you reach a goal, like finding a new job, or to pull you back from the brink of helplessness like our gratitude ritual initially did for us, having a daily ritual is one of the most powerful things you can do to help you change your life for the better.

The little things you do daily—your rituals—define you. All the progress you make in your life from this moment forward will come from your rituals. Take this to heart!

Goals and Rituals

As Marc was watching the Academy Awards one night at a friend's house, he noticed something that many of the acceptance speeches had in common. It went something like: "This means so much to me. My whole life has been leading up to this moment."

Think about that for a second. Every single thing you've gone through in life—every high, every low, and everything in between—has led you to the moment you're experiencing right now. This means that you are exactly where you need to be to get to where you want to go. It's just a matter of taking one new step in the right direction, and another, and another.

So start with a simple question: how will you get where you want to go? Whether you're hoping someday to be happier or in better physical shape, or become a runner, a writer, an artist, a graphic designer, a programmer, a teacher, a better parent, a

> The universe isn't going to make your desires come true. You are.

successful entrepreneur, or an expert in a particular field, what's your road map to get there? Do you write your intention on a note card, then place it in a bottle and cast it out to sea, hoping the universe reads it and manifests it in your life? No. The universe isn't going to make your desires come true. You are. Do you set yourself a concrete goal to complete within a year, or within three years? Perhaps, but that alone doesn't get the job done. In fact, if you think back on previous examples in your life, setting lofty, long-term goals probably hasn't worked for you very often. How many times has this strategy led to the outcome you desired?

Here's the truth: goals don't make positive changes happen, daily rituals do.

So whether you currently find yourself in a rut or in the midst of a major crisis, or you simply long to get started on those goals you've put on the back burner, real change starts with what you do today. Tomorrow. Every day. Like the first step that every great journey begins with, rituals will get you going—and get you there.

Like many people, we learned this lesson the hard way. We spent years struggling to make even the slightest bit of progress on the goals we had set for ourselves, which were all just milestones we had created to help us get back to happy. We started new workout programs with great optimism, at least a couple of dozen times. We threw away all the junk food in our house more times than we can even remember. We tried waking up earlier, meditating, reading more often, writing a book, getting out of debt, running a business, and more . . .

But for the longest time we failed on all fronts. We'd get started with a new goal, then we'd get derailed, and boy, did we feel horrible! We often felt like losers—that no matter how hard we tried, our goals were out of reach. We'd berate ourselves constantly for not being stronger, smarter, and more disciplined.

But what we didn't realize then is that it was never a matter of not having enough strength, intelligence, or discipline. It was a matter of focusing on our goals in an ineffective way.

In fact, believe it or not, we were actually focusing on our goals *too* much. Yes, you read that right. It sounds counterintuitive, but it's the truth. Too often we obsess over a big goal, something we desperately want in our life, but are completely unfocused when it comes to the ritual—the recurring steps—that ultimately makes the goal attainable. So the weight of this big unrealized goal sits heavily on our mind, slows our progress to a crawl, and perpetuates our unhappiness.

Does that sound at all familiar? If so, it's time to shift your focus *away* from your goals and toward the rituals that support them. Let's take a closer look at the difference between a goal and a ritual:

- If you're a bodybuilder, your goal is to win a bodybuilding competition. Your ritual is what you do to train your body at the gym each day.
- If you're a novelist, your goal is to write a novel. Your ritual is the time you dedicate each day to putting your thoughts into words.

- If you're a parent, your goal is to be a great role model. Your ritual is the time and energy you commit to setting a good example each day.
- If you're a university student, your goal is to learn and earn a degree. Your ritual is your daily study habits.
- If you're a human being, your goal is to live a happy, meaningful life. Your ritual is the small, positive steps forward you take every day.

Now consider this: if you stopped focusing on one of your goals for a while and instead focused exclusively on your corresponding ritual, would you still make progress? For example, if you were trying to lose weight and you stopped thinking about your goal to lose twenty pounds, and instead placed all of your focus on eating healthy and exercising each day, would you still lose weight? Yes, without a doubt! Gradually you would get closer to your goal— your target weight—without even thinking about it again.

We're going to lay down the law here, based on more than a decade of experience helping our clients achieve the changes and results they desire. What we've learned from that experience is this: *nothing will change unless you make a daily ritual that reinforces your goal.* We've tried weekly action steps with people, things they do every other day, big monthly milestones, and dozens of other variations and combinations of strategies. And none of them work well in the long run—except daily rituals. If you're not willing to create a daily ritual to reinforce your goal, you don't really want to change your life as much as you say you do. You only like the *idea* of learning to be fit, writing a book, building a business, selling your art, getting back to happy, and so on. You don't actually want to do it every day.

Building Bulletproof Rituals

Rituals are meant to change your mindset about who you are as a person and broaden your belief in what you can accomplish. They offer a way to remain focused on the type of life you want to live, keeping your energy reserved for things that matter to you most. When considering what rituals you want to add to your routine, start by being mindful of what you want to change in your life. Choose any area you want to improve, and then:

1. Write down the specific details about your current circumstances. What's bothering you? What do you want to change?

2. Write down your answer to this question: What are the daily rituals that have contributed to your current circumstances? What are you doing that contributes to the situation you're in?

3. Write down the specific details about your ideal circumstances. What would make you happy?

4. Write down your answers to these questions: What are the daily rituals that will get you from where you are to where you want to be? What small daily steps will help you move forward?

Whenever we're struggling, we work through these four points and get valuable insight into where the negative rituals in our lives are coming from and what needs to change. Recently we found that much of our stress stemmed from our *always being in a rush*. We were constantly working, worried that we weren't getting enough done. We missed out on quality time with each other and with our son; we often looked at social media even before giving each other a good morning kiss.

We decided that to change this trend—this negative ritual— we needed to have a calmer start to each day, so the small change we made was to slow down and implement new positive rituals into our morning routines. Rather than wake up and immediately turn to emails and social media, we stay away from the computer. We take time for ourselves. We drink a glass of water—yes, the ritual can be as simple as that—and make a cup of tea, allowing time to begin the day in a more mindful state.

When you make the commitment to begin practicing a ritual, no matter what it is, think of it as a lifestyle change that you'll be doing for the long term. To really drive home the importance of considering your rituals as lifestyle changes, we think of Angel's mother, Mary, and her commitment to working out. She was struggling with going to the gym every day, a problem most of us with busy schedules have. She was following the stereotypical pattern of taking on too much all at once, trying to spend as much as one and a half or even two hours at the gym each day. Sure enough, she started to come up with excuses for the days she couldn't get to the gym.

So instead, we suggested that she go to the gym for just fifteen minutes every day. Initially, she balked at this idea. But when we told her to think of going to the gym as a long-term goal—not just a getting-skinny-for-a-high-school-reunion goal—she reconstructed the ritual in her head. With our help, she began to establish ways in which she could ensure her lifestyle changes were implemented, and her gym ritual has stuck.

The Keys to Building and Implementing a Ritual

Now, you might be thinking, "But where do I start, really? And how do I stick to a new ritual?" We talked about the difference between a goal and a ritual, and how to turn the former into the latter—how to make it actionable and recurring. There are a few more things to know about creating a ritual routine that works, so let's dive in.

Rituals are meant to serve you for the long term, and they aren't meant to stress you out. So it's important to do it right. The ritual-building rules and tips we're about to share here are fairly simple, but if you stick to them diligently, they're basically infallible. These three guidelines are critical, and they have to do with making your rituals manageable: that is, start with one ritual, make it small, and maintain it for at least sixty days.

1. **Focus on one (and only one) positive change at a time.** You can break this rule, and sadly most people do, but don't be surprised if you fail because of it. If you try to do too much, nothing gets done right. So implement one positive change, and make it a ritual for a month before considering adding to it or starting a second. Only build upon your ritual if you are successful; otherwise, stay with it until it feels like second nature.

2. **Keep your ritual small to start.** You've probably heard this before, but again, most people don't do it. Start with a daily ritual that lasts fifteen minutes or less. If you feel strong resistance and fail at fifteen minutes, drop it to five or even three minutes, and then do it for a full month before adding more time.

3. **Remember that establishing a ritual takes time.** We tell our clients they need sixty days for a new ritual to become a part of their lives. By then they identify with it. This perspective shift is enormously important. They start to see the positive change they've implemented in their life, and they feel rewarded as they watch it shape them into a better, calmer person.

With these three keys implemented, here are five additional tools you can use to support your efforts and make sure you continue to practice your rituals.

Set up Positive Triggers

Maya Angelou only wrote in small hotel rooms. Jack Kerouac made sure to touch the ground nine times before sitting down to write. And many of the artistic clients and students we've worked with over the years have done everything from meditating, to singing, to running, to even doing two-hour-long workouts immediately before working on their creative projects.

For example, take a look at our client Fay's morning routine. Fay told us how she begins each day with a simple series of actions, inspired by Twyla Tharp's book *The Creative Habit*, which she implemented after we challenged her to set up triggers for her daily workout ritual. She wakes up at 6:00 a.m., puts on her workout clothes, walks outside her downtown San Francisco home, hails a taxi, and tells the driver to take her to the gym. She works out for forty-five minutes, then takes a leisurely fifteen-minute jog back home.

The key to Fay's ritual is the morning cab ride, which serves as a trigger that helps lock in her morning workout and keep her on track. Fay says: "The most important part of the ritual is not the training I do at the gym; what's important is getting into that cab every morning and getting the day started in the right direction. The rest just falls into place. I get home feeling good and ready to work."

Think about your days. How are they structured? What triggers your creative and productive mind? Are you consciously structuring your days with this trigger in mind? Whether it's waking up early, working in a specific location, or hitting the weights first thing in the morning, you need to find a trigger that gets you into a rhythm—*your* rhythm. When you design a healthy daily routine that starts automatically every morning, you save lots of mental energy for the thinking and productivity that comes naturally when you find yourself in your rhythm. Through this personalized routine, you will be able to bring out your most intuitive work.

Of course, your routine will change occasionally due to evolving circumstances. The idea is that you make the necessary adjustments and maintain a routine that works, one with the right triggers and rituals to develop and nurture your mind so you can do the work necessary to get you from where you are to where you want to be.

Don't Break the Chain

We've mentioned that a ritual is something you do every single day. This can be challenging, especially if you're just starting out. If you're unsure what triggers might be most effective for you, consider one we call "Don't break the chain." It's an easy visual trigger that motivates you to keep going and remain on track. Let's say the ritual you want to implement is journaling every day. Set up a desk calendar or a wall calendar and mark an X on the days you've written in your journal. The idea here is that you can look at your calendar and quickly see evidence of your progress and of what needs to be done today.

If you're two weeks into the ritual, journaling every night, marking your calendar, it's going to be more difficult to ignore the chain of Xs on your calendar. However tired you might be, the calendar is your daily inspiration. You'll find yourself asking: is it really that time-consuming to write down two sentences about my day and what I'm grateful for? As a form of visual motivation, we think it's a simple and effective way to hold yourself accountable for implementing the change you want in your life. Your daily rituals sometimes need a little extra push to keep you going, and this will do just that.

Create Visual Reminders

You want to lose weight, but when you're tired, it's easy to rationalize that you'll start exercising and eating right tomorrow. You want to build a more profitable business, but when you're caught up in the daily grind, it's easy just to do what's familiar instead of what's required for growth. You want to nurture your closest relationships, but when you're busy, it's easy to rationalize that you really need to work on that client proposal instead. Few good things come easy, and when the going gets tough, we often take the easy way out—even though the easy way usually takes us the wrong way.

To combat this, create tangible reminders that pull you back from your weak impulses. A friend of ours who has paid off almost a hundred thousand dollars of debt in the past five years has a copy of his credit card balance taped to his computer monitor; it serves as a constant reminder of the debt he wants to pay off. Another friend keeps a photo of herself when she was ninety pounds heavier on her refrigerator as a reminder of the weight she never wants to be again. And another fills his desk with family photos, both because he loves looking at them and because when work gets really tough, these photos remind him of the people he is ultimately working for.

Think of moments when you are most likely to give in to impulses that take you away from your goals and the rituals you need to get there. Then use visual reminders of those goals to interrupt the impulse and keep you on track.

Establish Accountability

One of the most important tools for being successful with your rituals is accountability. We have worked with hundreds of coaching clients over the years, and what drives them to success is having someone else hold them accountable for the ritual. The interesting thing about accountability, though, is that it can often feel like someone is badgering you. If someone calls you every day to ask whether or not you're continuing with a goal, you might begin to feel negative toward either the ritual or the person.

To avoid this, we came up with a system. At the beginning of each month, we both write down ten accountability questions that we want to ask ourselves during the upcoming month. The questions can differ slightly from month to month or they can remain the same, but they always pertain specifically to the rituals we've set in place for ourselves. For example, Marc's questions always include: *Did you spend an hour of uninterrupted time writing today? Have you spent fifteen minutes meditating today? Did you spend an hour being present with your son?* Once we've written down our questions, we exchange papers. Every day, we ask each other the questions— Angel asks Marc his questions, and Marc asks Angel her questions.

This way, it feels less like we're hounding each other, because these are the questions we'd ask of ourselves anyway.

Find a reliable accountability partner for yourself. They can be near or far—exchanging questions can be done via email—and talk to them every day. It doesn't matter how many questions you write down, but we recommend anywhere from five to ten. Asking yourself the questions helps you consider what rituals you want to implement in your life, and your accountability partner can better help you stick to them. You can even amplify the accountability by making a commitment to someone close to you that you're going to stick to your ritual. This could be your spouse, your best friend, or maybe even your dog. The key is to make the daily practice of your ritual akin to a promise to someone you hold dear, someone you don't want to let down. When following through with your ritual is also honoring a commitment to someone you care about, you'll be that much more motivated to practice that ritual every day.

Create Consequences for Slacking Off

The most significant consequence of not following through with your daily ritual is losing the respect of those to whom you have made a commitment. But you can also create other, slightly more fun consequences: Recently, Marc made a promise to a group of friends that he would donate a hundred dollars to a political campaign he's not fond of each time he didn't follow through with his commitment. He hasn't missed his commitment yet. He also made a promise to eat octopus sushi if he slacked off. (And he won't, because eating raw octopus is repulsive to him—like eating a rat.) He's promised to sing embarrassing karaoke songs in front of strangers if he fails. The consequences can also be positive—a reward each week if you don't miss a day, for example. Also, make the consequences more severe if you miss two days straight, and even more severe if you miss three.

Important Principles to Remember When Building Rituals

Some of these principles may be new to you, and others you will have heard a hundred times, but *all* are absolutely worth remembering.

Accepting Some Level of Discomfort Is Necessary

Starting a new daily ritual forces us to change our routine in some way, and this change, by its nature, is somewhat uncomfortable. But most of us don't want to be uncomfortable, so we run from the possibility of discomfort constantly. The obvious problem with this is that by running from discomfort, we are constrained to participate in only the activities and opportunities within our comfort zones. And since our comfort zones are relativity small, we miss out on most of life's greatest and healthiest experiences, and we get stuck in a debilitating cycle with our goals. We keep doing what we've always done, and thus we keep getting the results we've always gotten. And our true potential falls by the wayside.

Small Rituals Are Much *Easier to Start and Maintain*

Making a big change all at once requires not only lots of grit and determination, but also lots of time and energy. And if you already have a reasonably busy schedule, you'll find it hard to fit a new daily ritual into the mix. You might do it once or twice—exercise for an hour, for example—but then the new ritual gets put on hold because you feel like you don't have enough time. That's why a small change—perhaps a small ritual that consists of just ten sit-ups every morning when you get out of bed—is much easier to start and maintain.

The truth is that enthusiasm always wanes a couple of days after you start a new ritual, but it's 100 percent easier to keep it going when the ritual is small. And keeping it going is what matters.

Ultimately, You Want to Expand Your Idea of "Normal"

We get comfortable with a certain set of conditions, and if we deviate from these conditions too quickly, we tend to get overwhelmingly uncomfortable. Quitting your day job and building a business, for example, requires you to figure out your finances, design and test products and services, write marketing material, set up a website, design sales funnels, and so on. All of this can be very daunting at the beginning. But if building this business is a goal you truly want to achieve, you have to do these things, and you have to start before you feel "ready."

The key again is leveraging daily rituals to ease into these uncomfortable requirements. Start with figuring out your finances—paying off debt, saving up a year's worth of living expenses, etc. Then, once you're comfortable in that area, decide on a product or service idea (daily market research), then set up your website (in small daily steps), write some marketing copy (again, in small daily steps), learn about Facebook marketing, run some ads on Facebook to test the marketability of your product or service. Ease into each part of your new business, and all its requirements gradually become part of the conditions that you're familiar with—your new and expanded "normal."

Renewing Your Trust in Yourself Is Imperative

What Angel and I lacked before we learned to build goal-achieving daily rituals was the trust that we were actually capable of achieving our goals. We had failed so many times in the past, and had grown so discouraged with ourselves, that we started choosing procrastination over trying to fulfill the goal-oriented promises we made to ourselves. In essence, we lost trust in both our abilities and ourselves. It's kind of like another person constantly lying to you—eventually you stop trusting them. The same holds true with the promises you make to yourself that always end in disappointment—eventually you stop trusting yourself. And the solution in most cases is the same too: you have to renew your trust gradually, with small promises, small steps (your daily rituals), and small victories. This takes time, but it happens pretty fast if you stick to it. And it's arguably one of the most important things you can do for yourself.

Small, Incremental Changes
Quickly Become Huge Changes

The concept of taking it one step at a time might seem ridiculously obvious, but at some point we all get caught up in the moment and find ourselves yearning for instant gratification. We want what we want, and we want it now! And this yearning often tricks us into taking on too much too soon. Angel and I have seen this transpire hundreds of times over the years: a coaching client or course student wants to achieve a big goal (or ten) all at once, and can't choose just one or two daily rituals to focus on, so nothing worthwhile ever gets done. Let this common mistake—this quick-fix mentality—be your reminder.

You can't lift a thousand pounds all at once, yet you can easily lift one pound a thousand times. Small, repeated, incremental efforts will get you to your goal. It doesn't happen in an instant, but it does happen a lot faster than not getting there at all.

A Few More Great Ideas to Build Your Own Rituals

By now we hope you have some ideas about the specific changes you want to create in your life, and a bunch of tools to help you create the rituals that will help you make those changes. To give you even more of a boost, here are some simple ideas for powerful rituals you can implement right now. You may also use these ideas to create new rituals of your own that will help you start thinking better and getting back to happy.

Implement Gratitude Mantras

Sometimes, on the hardest of days, we still have a tough time mustering up enough positive energy to maintain our rituals and focus on things to be grateful for. When this happens, we review our notes on gratitude, the perspectives and lessons we've learned over the years that we've documented in various archived blog posts. We call these notes our gratitude mantras. And on those days when everything seems to be going wrong, we will read through and reflect on them for as long as it takes for us to find a source of gratitude.

These are examples of mantras we use, and we pass them on to you in hopes that you will find refuge in them as well. Repeat them to yourself and reflect on them in those dark moments when you've lost track of your own rituals.

- When life gives you every reason to be negative, think of one good reason to be positive. There's always something to be grateful for.
- The greatest secret to happiness and peace is letting every life situation be what it is, instead of what you think it should be, and then making the very best of it.
- Choose to smile today by taking life moment by moment, complaining very little, and being thankful for the little things that mean a lot.
- No, you won't always get what you want. But remember this: there are lots of people who will never have what you have right now.
- Happiness comes a lot more easily when you stop complaining about your problems and start being grateful for all the problems you don't have.
- Never let all the things you want make you forget about all the things you have. Today, focus on exactly what you have, not on what you haven't.
- Be grateful for your life. For your health, your family, your friends, and your home. Many people don't have these things.

Using these mantras and paying attention to what we are grateful for reminds us why we have our rituals in the first place. If you aren't mindful of your situation, then how are you going to know whether or not you need to change it?

Spend Daily Downtime Daydreaming

Despite what your grade school teachers likely told you, day-dreaming is anything but a waste of time. While structured routines are important for the actual process of being productive, our minds need downtime filled with the freedom to wander, and you can build rituals for exactly this purpose.

Neuroscientists have found that daydreaming involves the same brain processes associated with imagination and creative thinking. According to psychologist Rebecca McMillan, who coauthored a research paper titled "Ode to Positive Constructive Daydreaming," daydreaming can aid in the "creative incubation" of ideas and solutions to complex problems. Perhaps that's why we sometimes get our best ideas while taking a long, hot shower.

Scheduling time for a daydreaming ritual might seem counter-intuitive, but we're programmed to spend the majority of our time in productivity mode. We know it can take awhile to unlearn the habit. When you're used to your days being a constant flurry of activity, you might feel strange or even guilty for allowing yourself some time to do nothing at all. But once you carve out space for it in your everyday life, daydreaming comes naturally—the hardest part is simply allowing yourself the downtime in the first place. And once you realize it's perfectly acceptable to let yourself breathe and relax, then you can lie back and let your thoughts flow. You'll be amazed by the ideas you come up with when you allow yourself time to decompress and dream.

Schedule New Experiences

Learn to love new experiences, sensations, and states of mind. This willingness to stretch yourself is a significant predictor of your output potential, because growth always begins at the edge of your comfort zone. Of course, a big part of this happens inside a routine when you're "in rhythm" and working hard to stretch your creative and intellectual muscles. But new experiences help balance out your routines. They force you to think differently. When you're placed in a new situation, you realize certain things you are capable of as a human being. Just as sticking to rituals can make you feel more accomplished and mindful of your capabilities, so can new experiences.

Make an effort to build a ritual that involves trying something new at least once a week. It can be a whole new activity, such as rock climbing or taking a dance class, or a small experience, such as talking to a stranger. Once you begin, many of these new experiences will open doors to life-changing perspectives you can't even fathom right now. And with a strategy of continuous small, scheduled steps into new experiences, you'll be able to sidestep the biggest barrier to thinking outside the box: fear.

Refocus on the Positive

Sometimes you have to give your wandering mind a little help by consciously selecting something positive to think about. Any positive thought will do to refocus your attention. When things are going well, and you're in a good mood, this is fairly easy. When times are tough, however, and your mind is flooded with negativity, this can be a real challenge. In these moments, think about your day and identify one positive thing that happened, no matter how small. If you can't think of something from today, reflect on the previous day, or even another recent time. The point here is to have something positive, no matter how small, that you're ready to shift your attention to when negativity starts to stir in your mind.

As Shawn Achor describes in his book *The Happiness Advantage,* a recent scientific study showed that doctors who are put in a positive mood before making a diagnosis consistently experience significant boosts to their intellectual abilities compared to doctors in a neutral state, which allows them to make accurate diagnoses almost 20 percent faster. The same study also examined people in other vocations, and found that optimistic salespeople outsell their pessimistic counterparts by more than 50 percent. Students primed to feel happy before taking math tests substantially outperform their neutral peers. It turns out that our minds are hardwired to perform at their best not when they are negative, or even neutral, but when they are positive.

Of course, that's not to say that you should never get upset, but you'll be a more effective human in all sorts of ways if you can create a daily ritual that enables you to mindfully accept and let go of negative emotions rather than dwell on them. So try to focus a little less on managing your problems, and a little more on managing your mindset. Keep it positive!

Practice Mindful Relaxation Techniques

Mindful relaxation is the key to mental and physical recuperation. There are many ways to do this, but the foundation of all of them is focused breathing (a form of meditation). Your breath is the bridge between your life circumstances and your consciousness— it unites your body and your thoughts. So when you're feeling stressed, take a ten-minute break to sit quietly and focus on your breathing. Close the door, put away all other distractions, and just sit in a chair with your eyes closed and breathe.

The goal with this ritual is to spend the entire time focused only on the feeling of your chest rising and falling, which will prevent your worried mind from wandering and overthinking. This sounds simple, but it's challenging to do for more than a minute or two, especially when you're just starting out with this ritual. And it's perfectly fine if random thoughts sidetrack you; this is sure to happen, and you just need to bring your focus back to your breathing.

Bottom line: whenever your thoughts become scattered by stress and busyness, use your breath as a means to take hold of your mind. Just breathe and be present for a moment; you'll feel better.

Have Calm, Consistent Morning Routines

Too many books and courses on personal success act like we're robots, and completely overlook the enormous power of our emotions. The less frenzied our emotions are at the start of the day, the calmer they will be all day. When we start the day in a peaceful, mindful state, it's easy to focus and get the right things done. But when you wake up and stress is already upon you—phones ringing, emails and texts dinging, problems arising—you spend the whole day reacting instead of being proactive. This means you're not working on your priorities—the things that drive you toward success—but simply responding to whatever gets thrown at you, whether it's important to you or not.

To counteract this, make the first hour of your day a ritual in its own right, and try to vary it as little as possible. A trusted routine can be extremely effective in helping you feel in control and non-reactive, which reduces anxiety and stress, and therefore makes you more mindful and competent. The routine can differ for everyone; ours is one in which we wake before our son, so we can anticipate and prepare for his needs. Then we'll have coffee and do our morning meditation. Angel will often read a book that inspires her to begin the day while I do my morning stretch routine. These rituals work effectively for us.

Pay attention to how you operate best. What is going to put you in a state of mind that allows you to truly take on the day?

How you start your day has an enormous impact on your overall effectiveness. Keep it simple and free of stress. Once you've committed to your calm morning routine, you're going to reap the benefits of a calmer, proactive work day. (We talk more about morning routines later in this chapter.)

Eliminate Needless Busywork

At some point we all wonder, "Why is it so impossible to get everything done?" But the answer is stunningly simple: we're doing too many of the wrong things. And if you want to build in rituals that will make a difference in your life, it can help to reduce or eliminate some of the day-to-day tasks that may seem important but are actually getting in the way.

Several research studies have shown that people never get more done by blindly working extra hours on everything that comes up. Instead, they're more productive when they follow careful plans that measure and track key priorities and milestones. So if you want to be more successful in life, don't ask how to make something more efficient until you've first asked, "Do I need to do this at all?"

If you think about it, it's actually kind of ironic that we complain we have so little time, and then we prioritize like time is infinite. So do your best to focus on what's truly important, and not much else. Pay attention to your goals and keep track of where you want to go.

Keep a Personal Notebook

Oprah keeps a journal. Eminem keeps a journal. J. K. Rowling keeps a journal. Happy people track their progress, set goals, reflect, and learn from their mistakes. And they often use some kind of notebook to accomplish this. If you want to get somewhere in life, you need a map, and your notebook is that map. You can write down what you did today, what you tried to accomplish, where you made mistakes, and so forth. It's a place to reflect. It's a place to capture important thoughts. It's a place to track where you've been and where you intend to go. It's one of the most underused yet incredibly effective tools out there, and it's available to anyone.

Keeping a journal is an excellent way to combine several of the rituals we talked about above. In many ways, it's a one-stop shop. You can remind yourself of what you're grateful for by listing all of the things in your life that matter to you now. You can record your daydreaming ideas in your journal and fine-tune them. You can use your journal as a place to reflect on a podcast you heard or a book you read that spoke to you. Writing down daily inspiration refocuses your mind on what is truly important to you and eliminates your desire to spend your time focusing on negative, time-consuming habits. The journal might even become such an important part of your life that you'll feel strange without it.

The Power of Good Morning Rituals

A good morning, and thus a good day, isn't an experience that just magically happens—it's created consciously. Yet most of us are distracted from the start every morning, and therefore stumble through each day with diminished intention and lots of unnecessary frustration. We forget that the morning hours leading up to midday are enormously important; these hours form the foundation of the entire day. We forget that how we choose to spend this time on a daily basis can be used to predict the kind of days we're going to have, and ultimately the kind of lives we're going to live. So trivial activities—checking social media, watching TV, worrying about things we can't control—typically set the tone of each day. Which means we waste lots of well-rested time and energy on little things that don't matter, while gradually losing touch with the significant, controllable parts of our lives that actually do matter.

On the other hand, having thoughtful, deliberate morning hours—generally from the time we wake up until noon—allows us to reestablish a sense of meaningful control, to put ourselves back in control so we can start to live more intentional, effective lives again.

Little Life-Changing Things (Rituals) to Do Before Noon

Why before *noon,* and not earlier? Because not all of us get up at the crack of dawn. Not all of us have the same schedules. And you certainly don't have to be on someone else's schedule to fit these three life-changing rituals into your mornings. The key is to get them done in the morning hours of your day, before the drag of the afternoon gets the best of you.

And please note the mention of "gradually" above. If you aren't doing any of these things before noon right now, start with just the first one, then try adding the second down the road . . .

1. **Wash your dishes as soon as you finish breakfast every morning.**

    You *are* eating the most important meal of the day, right? Good. Now you can leverage your breakfast to strengthen your self-discipline.

    Start small every morning. Very small. By simply washing your dishes after breakfast.

Yes, we mean literally washing your dishes with your own two hands. It's just one little step forward every morning: When you eat your oatmeal, wash your bowl and spoon. When you finish drinking your morning coffee, rinse the coffeepot and your mug. Don't leave any dirty dishes in the sink or on the counter for later. Wash them immediately.

Form this ritual one dish at a time, one morning at a time. Once you do this consistently for a few weeks, you can start wiping down the sink. Then the counter. Then make your bed. Pack yourself a healthy lunch. Start doing sit-ups and meditate for a few minutes (more on these two below). And so forth.

Practice the aforementioned consistently and you'll start to build a healthy ritual of self-discipline. You'll finally know yourself to be capable of doing what must be done, with focus and intention.

But for the next few weeks, start by washing the breakfast dishes, mindfully.

2. **Use exercise for fifteen minutes or less to train your body and mind.**

Exercise is the simplest and fastest way to change your life, not only because it strengthens the body, but because it also strengthens the mind. And it almost instantaneously instills a positive sense of self-control into the subconscious, even when other circumstances in life seem chaotic.

In this way, exercise becomes a personal space where you are able to train and regain control over your own world. Only you can move your body. Only you can push yourself to step forward. Only you get to choose your level of intensity. When you start your day like this—in control—the wider world is far easier to navigate.

Furthermore, a consistent daily exercise ritual changes the physical inner workings of your brain. In his bestselling book *Spark: The Revolutionary New Science of Exercise and the Brain,* Dr. John Ratey discusses data he collected through years of researching the neurological changes exercise causes in the human brain. He states, "Exercise is the single most powerful tool you have to optimize your brain function. Aerobic activity has a dramatic effect on adaptation, regulating systems that might be out of balance and optimizing those that are not—it's an indispensable tool for anyone who wants to reach his or her full potential."

We have come to very similar, although less scientific, conclusions on our own too. With more than a decade of experience working individually with clients, we have found that exercise truly is a universal medicine for most human disorders and challenges. It drastically reduces mild and moderate depression, eases anxiety, counterbalances the negative effects of being overstressed, and more. And exercise is obviously not just a mental workout, but a physical one as well: you're achieving two aims at once.

So if exercise is that wonderful, why are we recommending *only* fifteen minutes of it each morning? Because starting small is key. We know you've heard this before, but again, so many of us forget to follow good advice. Start with a morning ritual of exercise that lasts fifteen minutes or less. If you feel strong resistance at fifteen minutes, drop it to ten minutes, or seven minutes, and then stick to it for at least a full month before increasing the duration again.

3. **Establish presence through meditation (for fifteen minutes or less).**

     The same timeless principle of starting small applies here as well. However, a morning meditation ritual of only fifteen minutes is no easy feat for most beginners. During the first several attempts, most novice meditators tend to find it near impossible to quiet their minds. Because of this, many of us try meditation once or twice and do not see the value; it does not immediately instill the same sense of control over ourselves and our world that exercise does. But with practice and patience, meditation can be *far* more powerful. And that's why we both meditate every morning before breakfast.

     Meditation provides a deeper level of control that ultimately teases out of us what has been trapped inside— it connects us with our truest selves by allowing us to access all the areas of our mind and body from which we are usually distracted and disconnected.

     The most basic, practical benefits of meditation are twofold:

*   It lowers mental stress.
*   It increases mental presence (awareness).

     And when we bring a more relaxed presence into our morning, it makes everything that happens from there much easier to deal with. Because we take the next step more mindfully, without pent-up resistance, fully aware and accepting of the tenseness in our shoulders, the little bubble of hope in our heart, or maybe even the haze of sadness in the back of our mind. And with this awareness and acceptance we find better solutions, healthier ways to cope, and a general sense that people are friendlier and days are brighter.

Conversely, when we are stressed out and distracted in the morning, our mind is split and frayed. One part is firmly focused on whatever is pressing in upon us, while the other part is giving minimal attention to whatever tasks need to be done quickly in the meantime. Imagine that you are late for work and you're rushing around your house preparing to leave. If a loved one starts telling you something important about what they are going to do today, how much of your attention is going to be focused on what they are telling you? Not much.

But when we become more present—when we gradually establish more awareness and acceptance of the present through meditation—we stop being as distracted and preoccupied. In the space that opens, we can breathe deeply and listen deeply. For a moment, stress slips off our shoulders. And with practice we can learn to have more and more presence and peacefulness in our life.

A course student of ours recently summed it up perfectly in an email to us: *"Every moment is a new opportunity. The next one is as fresh and full of promise as the thousand before that you missed, and it is completely empty of any judgment whatsoever. Nothing is carried over that you take with you. You don't have to pass a good-person exam before you enter; it is totally*

unconditional. It's as if it is saying, 'Okay, so you missed me the
last ten thousand moments, but look! Here I am again . . . and
again . . . and again!' And you are welcomed with open arms."

Here's how to establish presence through morning
meditation (note that while there are many meditation
techniques, this is the one we are presently practicing): sit
upright in a chair with your feet on the ground and your
hands resting comfortably on your lap, close your eyes, and
focus on your breathing for fifteen minutes (or less in the
beginning if you prefer). The goal is to spend the entire
time focused only on the feeling of your chest inhaling
and exhaling, which will prevent your worried mind from
wandering and overthinking. This sounds simple, but again,
it's challenging to do for more than a couple of minutes,
especially when you're just starting out with this ritual.
And it's perfectly fine if random thoughts sidetrack you—
this is sure to happen. You just need to bring your focus
back to your breathing.

Remember, Consistency Is Everything

The three morning rituals we've just discussed mean nothing if they
are not practiced consistently. One morning of cleaning your dishes,
exercising, and meditation by itself won't cut it. It is the gradual com-
pounding of simple and seemingly minor actions over weeks,
months, and years that leads to life-changing, positive results. There
is nothing noticeably special about putting one foot in front of the
other every day for weeks, but by doing so, many normal human
beings have climbed over twenty-nine thousand feet to the top of
the highest mountain in the world, Mount Everest. There is nothing
noticeably special about cleaning dishes, exercising, or sitting quietly

in meditation for a short time every morning, but by doing so, we enjoy much better lives.

You have a choice today. Prove to yourself, in little ways every morning, that you have the power to take control of your day and your life.

We won't lie to you: establishing rituals requires dedication. It's you telling yourself every day that you *can* do this, and that there is no better day than today to start. It's about paying attention to the negative pursuits that are taking you away from the practices that can help you better your life. It's about examining yourself, and having the courage to enact a positive change right away. We know what it's like to be stuck in our ways, to take the path of least resistance, and to keep doing things the way we always have. It's hard—especially when times are hard—but we are here to tell you that it's worth it. When you make the commitment to practice your rituals consistently, you'll be amazed by how much you accomplish. So start with a simple ritual that works for you, and stick to it.

Closing Exercise

It's been suggested that we judge a man by his questions rather than by his answers. This is such sound advice, because if you keep asking yourself the wrong questions, you will never get an answer you like.

On a piece of paper, write down at least five rituals you believe you practice every day. They can be both positive and negative. The key here is to be deliberate and mindful. Evaluate each of these rituals by asking yourself a few questions that will help you better understand the purpose of those rituals in your life and reflect on whether or not they add or subtract from your well-being:

- Who am I when I practice this ritual?
- Is this ritual bringing me closer to or further from where I want to be?
- How is it helping me grow?
- How is it hurting me?
- What's the next positive step I can take with this ritual?

Do you see the power in simply asking yourself these questions? You won't know what rituals you want to implement in your life until you sit down and reflect on where you are now. So let this be a little wake-up call. Instead of looking outside yourself for answers, start asking yourself the right questions. They will serve as guideposts that have a powerful influence on the direction of your life. This kind of self-inquiry can help you stay true to your principles, pursue your desires, grow through adversity, and add value to the world around you. And it's the rituals you create from that self-inquiry that will allow you to start making progress.

CHAPTER 2

Mindfulness: Ease Out of Busyness and Into Awareness

Peace does not mean to be in a place
where there is no noise, trouble, or hard work.
Peace means to be in the midst of all those things
and still be calm in your heart.

On a chilly January morning just inside the entrance to a Washington, D.C., subway station, a young man took his violin out of its case and brought it up to his shoulder. He was dressed in regular clothes—just jeans and a T-shirt. And although he had a face many people might find attractive, on this particular morning it was mostly obscured by a dark baseball cap and shaggy brown hair. After plucking the strings for a couple of minutes to tune his instrument, he reached into his pocket and pulled out a few dollar bills, which he tossed into the violin case in front of him, hoping a few passersby would do the same. It was a busy morning in the subway station as the young man began to play. Thousands of people were busy hurrying to work, school, or wherever they were headed. Trains were coming and going—the morning rush was in full swing. Yet through all the busyness, the incredible sound of this young man's violin filled the subway station.

It was impossible to ignore. Or was it?

Over the course of forty-three minutes, more than a thousand people walked through the doors of the subway entrance where Joshua Bell was playing. And if he had been any other street performer, perhaps it would have been insignificant that he earned the attention of only a few people and just a handful of change. But Joshua Bell isn't just any street performer. He is possibly the world's most renowned violinist, and was playing one of the most difficult classical masterpieces ever composed. And that masterpiece was being played on a $3 million (yes, *million*) violin that emitted one of the purest, most eloquent sounds in the world.

Yet almost nobody noticed. Why? Because everyone was too busy hurrying to pause and notice the music.

Busyness Is a Crutch

Too much to do, not enough time to do it. Sound familiar? How often is "I'm busy" your excuse? It used to be Marc's excuse every day. Like those one thousand people who ran past Joshua Bell's music without a moment to spare, Marc had a schedule that left zero time for unplanned presence and awareness.

And he was proud of his busyness. He treated it like an accomplishment worth bragging about! He wanted to remind everyone how tough he had it. He wanted you to know how arduous it was to live in a beautiful suburban neighborhood and commute around town, not to mention how he had to juggle business and family. He'd tell you how he had to help our course students, coaching clients, and readers, then immediately rush out to the grocery store.

And he would only have a short time to get our son fed, settled, and bathed before bed each night. Marc could have gone on and on . . .

"Don't you see how busy I am? Don't you see it, everybody? Keep it in mind! Please!"

Yes, that's exactly what Marc used to want you to know about him. But not anymore. Now he pauses to hear the music.

He gradually learned the truth: busyness is *not* an accomplishment. Nothing worthwhile gets accomplished with a mindset that loves busyness for its own sake. This kind of busyness is a mindset that makes everything harder than it has to be. If we're not below the poverty line, juggling three jobs at once just to put food on the table, then our busyness is self-inflicted 98 percent of the time (the exception being that 2 percent of the time that a random series of incredibly difficult life events blindsides us).

Marc finally got a handle on his busyness after we studied it long enough to realize that yes, it was within our control. We came to realize that most of the time we actually created mad rushes and headaches where none were needed, and Marc was leading the pack. On a normal weekday, you would have found him running around nagging family, business associates, and basically everyone nearby to rush around with him.

"If you don't get your shoes tied faster, we're going to miss the movie!"
"If we don't get this task done in the next hour, we're never going to hit our target!"

The real kicker is, whether he provoked everyone to rush faster or not, we always collectively moved at about the same pace anyway. But when Marc pushed us all, everyone (including Marc) was unhappier. It became crystal clear that nearly all of his busyness was self-inflicted drama. He was creating it in his head as a reaction to unresolved thoughts, anxieties, and fears, and yet he subconsciously thought it would somehow make his life easier. Of course, it did the exact opposite: Marc's busyness only led to extra stress and complexity in our lives. And even on days when there really were lots of things to do—perhaps far too many things—it was almost always a matter of poor planning on his behalf.

Why was Marc making life harder, busier, and unhappier than it had to be? Sadly, a big reason so many of us fill our lives with needless busyness has to do with the always-plugged-in, always-connected, always-sharing, always-comparing society we live in. We default to defining ourselves based on where we are and what we have in relation to everyone else. If we don't have a "better" career, house, car, or pair of shoes, we feel inferior. And the only way we can possibly *do better* is to *be busier* doing . . . whatever!

After all, we are what we do, right? Job title, employer—aren't these typically the first things we share with strangers we meet at parties? We fill our social media feeds and our calendars with needless busyness to feel more accomplished—to avoid being just ourselves in the present moment. The cost? Our peace of mind, our sanity, and our happiness. We inevitably lose sight of what matters most, because our busyness has buried it with stress and the endless need to be somewhere else, doing something else, as fast as feasibly possible.

Twenty-five years ago, at the dawn of the modern internet revolution, people were predicting that our technological advancements would eventually allow us to work less, so we could pay more attention to what's truly important in our lives. Today, however, there's plenty of evidence to the contrary. We may be able to achieve twice as much in half the time, but that's what's expected of us now—it's the new baseline. On top of that, technology fills our free time with endless distractions—we're checking text messages, email, social media, etc., 24/7.

And so, despite its benefits, our technology has us feeling as desperately overwhelmed as ever.

The solution? Mindfulness. As a daily ritual, it's a way of living, of being, of seeing, of tapping into the full power of your humanity. At its core, mindfulness is:

- Being fully aware of what's going on in the present moment without wishing it were any better or any different.
- Appreciating each positive experience without holding on too tightly when things change (because inevitably things will change).
- Accepting each negative experience without fearing that life will always be that way (because it won't— again, everything changes).
- Eliminating all unnecessary distractions to focus on what matters most.
- Applying your full energy and attention in the present moment so you can then take practical action.

Before we started practicing mindfulness, we were being reactive rather than proactive. Each day we felt like we were running nonstop. We were struggling through adversity and coping with financial difficulties and the loss of loved ones. Income was tight, and with this came the urge to cram more things into the day, to save ourselves faster and be the heroes who wore busyness like a medal of accomplishment. There was always something else on the to-do list, always another thing that we thought deserved our attention more than the last. But rather than feel like we were getting everything together, we felt scattered and unfocused.

Once we made mindfulness a part of our lifestyle and took to implementing it as a ritual, however, an amazing calmness took over inside each of us. Positive energy started to flow, as a result of simply accepting that we were in the right place at the right time, regardless of where we were.

Implementing mindfulness trickles out into your everyday life. You begin to see that busyness is not a virtue. Most of our clients see busyness the way we once did: as productivity. But when you become mindful and ask yourself, *How can I take my most present, effective step forward?* you begin to realize what's truly important.

> Busyness is not a virtue.

Living every day in a way that makes mindfulness possible can be life changing. In the next section, we're going to help you get to that understanding by discussing ways to mindfully prioritize your time, let go of the desire to get everything done in one day, and reframe the way you view your busyness.

The Art of Mindfully Prioritizing

The moment we admit to ourselves that we're trying to cram too many things (tasks, obligations, distractions) into a relatively small space (twenty-four hours in a day), it becomes obvious that we need to clear some clutter from our schedules. Mindful prioritization is the key.

Pay close attention to all the things you do today—all the things you're trying to fit into twenty-four hours. How much TV are you watching in the morning and evening? What websites are you browsing? What games are you playing? How much time are you spending texting, emailing, or updating your social media accounts? How much online window shopping are you doing? How much time do you devote to eating, cleaning, and taking care of others? What else are you spending the precious minutes of your day on?

We aren't strangers to committing to doing too much in a single day. When we became parents, a huge learning curve came with having another person dictate our time. Angel shares how a little mindful prioritization helped declutter her schedule and her mind as a new mom:

> When Mac was born, the most challenging part came from having to compromise my time, especially since I was trying to do it all at once. When I was working, I was wishing I was with Mac. I was wondering what he was doing and worrying that I wasn't spending enough time with him. And then when I was with Mac, I was thinking of my to-do list and the work I wasn't getting done. It was a surprisingly challenging time for me; I was feeling torn in multiple directions, and I was never happy with where I was in the moment.
>
> Marc and I then started focusing on our presence and being happy with exactly where we were, and that made a huge difference. We prioritized our tasks. We made plans to have Marc's aunt come and watch Mac from 10:00 a.m. to 4:00 p.m. three days a week. This way, we could focus on work. We weren't worrying about Mac, because we knew he was in good hands, and we could spend our energy accomplishing the work tasks that needed to get done. This meant that when we were with Mac, we were enjoying it 100 percent. We weren't worrying about work, and this

all stemmed from prioritizing our tasks to better our ability to be in the moment.

What you might notice first when you start to dig into your busyness is that you're doing too many random things that don't need to be done—too many time wasters. Then you might also notice you're overcommitted, that too many obligations are filling up your life with needless stress and activity. You can start stealing back your time by eliminating as many nonessential distractions and obligations as possible, and saying no to new ones that arise. This is easier said than done, of course, but the important thing to realize is that you *can* change how you allocate your time.

First, look at your to-do list: how many of these things can you reasonably do in the next twenty-four hours? Probably only three to five, with sanity. Now consider this: which task would you work on if you could only work on one task over the next twenty-four hours? That is your number-one priority. Just that one task. The truth is, you probably can't complete everything on your list in one day's time, and you can't do your top three to five tasks right now. You can do only one thing at a time. So focus on your number-one task and, once you're done, then figure out what your next number-one task is. Clear everything else away and focus.

> You can do only one thing at a time.

Now that you have the general idea about how mindful prioritization works, here are a few guiding principles to keep in mind when it comes to mindfully prioritizing all the tasks in your life:

If you want to achieve a significant goal or outcome in your life, you have to give up the things that conflict with it. This doesn't mean you have to make your life unnecessarily grueling. It just means you can't have it all—you have to sacrifice something that you value less than whatever it is you ultimately want to achieve. So instead of thinking about what you want, first consider what you are willing to give up to get it. You can't have the destination without the journey. For example, if you want the six-pack abs, you have to also want the hard workouts and the healthy meals. So ask yourself: what is worth sacrificing for? This question shines a light on your true priorities. Because if you catch yourself wanting something day in and day out, month after month, yet you never take action and thus you never make any progress, then maybe you don't really want it after all, because you're not willing to suffer through the sacrifices and work it's going to take to achieve it. Maybe it's not actually a priority. Or if it is, maybe it's time to make some serious changes.

Overcommitting is the antithesis of living a peaceful, mindful life. There's a difference between being committed to the right things and being overcommitted to everything. It's tempting to fill every waking minute of the day with to-do list tasks or distractions. Don't do this to yourself. Leave space. Keep your life ordered and your schedule underbooked. Create a foundation with a soft place to land, a wide margin of error, and room to think and breathe.

When you try to control too much, you enjoy too little. Don't live a life packed full of ironclad plans. Work hard, but be flexible. The best moments are often unplanned, and the greatest regrets happen by not reaching exactly what was planned. Sometimes you just need to let go a little, relax, take a deep breath, and love what is right now.

When you are tired, you are attacked by negative circumstances you likely conquered long ago. An exhausted mind is an inefficient one. You must recharge on a daily basis. That means catching your breath, finding quiet solitude, focusing your attention inward, and otherwise making time to recuperate from the chaos of your routine. It's perfectly healthy to pause and let the world spin without you for a while. If you don't, you will likely burn yourself out by mulling over problems and circumstances that no longer need your attention.

The Art of Mindfully Deprioritizing

So what about all the other things you want to do (or feel you "should" do), that you simply can't get done? What do you do with the tasks that don't fit into twenty-four hours, or fit in at all? This is where the art of deprioritizing comes into play.

You can do those things tomorrow. Or you can decide to not do them at all. Either way, the reality is they won't fit into the next twenty-four hours of your life. And since these things were not top priorities, there's really no problem.

A problem only arises when you feel anxious, overwhelmed, and frustrated because you can't fit everything in. But you have to realize that the way you feel is based on your ideals—the thought that you should be able to do it all, be everything to everyone, and be superhuman—not your reality. So you have to adjust your ideals to match reality. And the reality is that you can't do everything. You can only choose to do some things—the important things—and everything else will have to wait, or get removed from your list.

We've taken to focusing on three core things every day: our clients and students, our writing, and our family. These are the things that are most important to us, so they're what we spend our energy and mindful presence focusing on. Once we started to do this, we were able to see the distractions for what they were. We could rule out the things we had only *thought* were obligations, because they didn't make it into our top priorities. And the sacrifices we had to make gradually came easier.

It's key to note that we're not scrambling to fit in twenty-five core things. If you have twenty-five things on your priority list, and they're all equally important to you, you're setting yourself up for mind*less*ness. It's impossible to get that many things done in one day, which leads to guilt and regret over the things you didn't achieve. That is the opposite of presence. Focus on what's truly important, and do what you can do today. Pick two, three, or five core things to focus on. That's enough. Deprioritize the rest and let go of thinking that it isn't.

Here are two reminders to help you through the process of mindfully deprioritizing the things that are keeping you from being present with what matters most.

Decide what you would put back on your plate if you could wipe it clean. Our lives get incredibly complicated, not overnight, but gradually. The complications creep up on us, one small step at a time.

How do we protect against this vicious cycle?

We have to take a step back on a regular basis and reevaluate:

What would you do if your schedule were empty? If your plate were completely clean, with limited space, what would you put on it today?

For Marc, he might add some quiet, focused writing time; playtime with our son; exercise time and tea time with Angel; a long lunchtime walk and a good afternoon talk with an old friend he hasn't spoken to in a while; a few short activities that matter to him and make a difference to others; reading and learning time; and time alone to think, meditate, and unwind before bed.

What would you choose to put on *your* plate?

Once you've figured that out, you just need to constantly look at invitations and activities and requests and tasks that pop up, and ask: is this one of the things I would choose to put on my clean plate?

And to help reinforce your decisions . . .

Learn to say *no*. Saying yes to everything puts you on the fast track to being miserable. Feeling like you're doing busywork is often the result of saying yes too often. We all have obligations, but a comfortable pace can only be found by properly managing your yeses. So stop saying yes when you want to say no. You can't always be agreeable. Sometimes you have to set clear boundaries.

You might have to say no to certain favors, or work projects, or community activities, or committees, or volunteer groups, or coaching your kid's sports team, or some other worthwhile activities.

You might be thinking that it seems unfair to say no when these are very worthwhile things to do. It kills you to say no. But you must. Because the alternative is that you're going to do a poor, halfhearted job at each one, be stressed beyond belief, and feel like you're stuck in an endless cycle of failure and frustration. You won't be getting enough sleep, your focus will get progressively worse due to exhaustion, and eventually you'll reach a breaking point.

So remember, the only thing that keeps so many of us stuck in this debilitating cycle is the fantasy in our minds that we can be everything to everyone, everywhere at once, and a hero on all fronts. But again, that's not reality. The reality is we're not Superman or Wonder Woman—we're human, and we have limits. We need to let go of the idea of doing everything and pleasing everyone and being everywhere at once. You're either going to do a few things well, or do everything poorly. That's the truth.

The Art of Mindfully Reframing

Once you have your priorities better managed, and you've deprioritized some things, it's time to reframe how you're generally thinking about the busyness that overwhelms you.

As human beings, how busy we *think* we are amplifies how overwhelmed we feel. That is, the stories we tell ourselves about life can either dramatically escalate or ease our stress levels. This is where reframing makes all the difference.

In a recent coaching session, Rebecca, a wife and mother of three who owns a successful photography business, told us about how she has reframed the way she thinks about her life:

> *I used to describe my life as overwhelming and busy, but not anymore. Now I see it as exceptionally rich and interesting. I feel empowered by the challenges I face personally and professionally.*

I'm not in denial, and I'm definitely exhausted at the end of most days. But it's now a satisfying kind of exhaustion. I did what I could do, and I did my best. And that makes me feel good. Of course, there are tough compromises that must be made some days, but that's okay—the compromises I must make just shine a light back on my priorities. I can't do it all. But I can do my best. I can do things for the right reasons. And I can make people feel respected and loved along the way.

By applying a new frame to the parts of her life she had previously described as overwhelming, Rebecca was able to see things in a fresh light: that she was doing her best, that she was doing things for the right reasons, and that her actions were helping others feel valued.

The Greek philosopher Epictetus said it perfectly more than two thousand years ago: "People are disturbed, not by things (that happen to them), but by the principles and opinions which they form concerning (those) things. When we are hindered, or disturbed, or grieved, let us never attribute it to others, but to ourselves; that is, to our own principles and opinions."

Modern behavioral science agrees too. American psychologist Albert Ellis, famous for developing rational emotive behavior therapy (REBT), has demonstrated that how people react to events is determined predominantly by their view of the events, not by the events themselves.

Sometimes changing your circumstances isn't possible, at least in the moment. You can't get a new job in an instant. You can't make someone else change against his or her will. And you certainly can't erase the past. But you absolutely *can* change your perception, belief, or opinion about your circumstances. Doing so will help you change your attitude and ultimately allow you to grow beyond the struggles you can't control.

The bottom line is that you always have options. Here are some reminders to help you mindfully reframe things and start to see your life as rich and interesting instead of overburdened.

Your only reality is *this moment*, right here, right now. The secret to health for the mind, body, and soul is not to mourn the past, or to worry about the future, but to live the present moment mindfully and purposefully. True wealth is the ability to experience the present moment fully. No other time and place is real. Lifelong peace and abundance can be found in such simple awareness.

A negative thought is harmless unless you believe it. It's not your thoughts, but *your attachment to your thoughts* that causes suffering. Attaching to a thought means believing it's true without proof. A belief is a thought that you've been attaching to, often for years.

You will not be punished for your anger; you will be punished by it. Speak and act when you are angry, and you will inevitably say something you will regret. Being angry and dramatic about something is easy. Doing something productive about it is the hard and worthwhile part. Life is too precious and too short to spend it being upset and dramatic. Drop it. Be positive. Be your best.

Inner peace is knowing how to belong to oneself, without external validation. In order to understand the world, you have to turn away from it on occasion. Sometimes the need to justify yourself to others causes you to cease to be at peace with your thoughts. Don't look for anyone else to give you permission to be yourself, or validation to be happy in the present moment.

Everything is created twice, first in your mind and then in your life. The real battle takes place in your mind first. If you're defeated in your thoughts, you've already lost. Remember this. Even if you have a good reason to be angry or resentful, don't. Channel your energy into thoughts and actions that actually benefit your life.

As we come to the end of this chapter, it's important to remind ourselves that the greatest enemy of good thinking and mindfulness is busyness. We all have seasons of wild schedules, but very few of us have a legitimate need to be busy *all* the time. Too often, we simply don't know how to prioritize well and say no when we should.

On the other hand, cultivating presence in any given moment allows us to focus on the things we *can* actually control, which is the key to getting back to happy. We've repeated this time and again: no matter what is happening in our lives, we can only fight the battles of today. Much of our stress, resentment, and worry stems from channeling our focus into the possibilities of other times and places outside of the here and now. Although being busy can make us feel more alive for a moment, whether tomorrow or on our deathbed, we will inevitably come to wish that we had spent less time in the buzz of busyness and more time actually living a purposeful, mindful life.

> We can only fight the battles of today.

Closing Exercise

In chapter 1, we talked about the importance of rituals, and having a daily ritual that helps you practice presence and mindfulness can pay huge dividends. Here are a few short mindfulness practices that will help you center yourself and be present, wherever you are and whatever your state of mind.

- Do a quick body scan. Focus on your body, and notice how each part of it feels right now. Do this for thirty seconds.
- Pay attention to your breath for sixty seconds. Listen to it, and feel it.
- Watch your thoughts about concerns, fears, judgments, doubts, and ideals for sixty seconds. Recognize that they are simply thoughts; you don't need to believe them or react to them.
- Walk mindfully, paying attention to your feet, your body, your breath, and your surroundings.

You can do each of these short mindfulness practices in little bits whenever you need them throughout your day. Remember, you don't have to meditate for thirty minutes to get the benefits of mindfulness. Just a couple of focused minutes of mindful attention can pay off hugely. The key is to make it a ritual, and do it every day.

Finally, if you need a little extra inspiration, here are seven reminders that help us stay present and keep things in perspective. When life gets hectic, and we feel overwhelmed, we reflect on these reminders for as long as it takes us to shift our mindset. We encourage you to do the same.

1. The best time to take a deep breath is when you don't feel like it—because that's when doing so can make the biggest difference.

2. Stress and feeling overwhelmed both come from the way you respond, not the way life is. Adjust your attitude, and these feelings will be gone. *You* control the way you look at life.

3. What you pay attention to grows. Focus exclusively on what matters, and let go of what does not.

4. It's okay. Show yourself some love. We can't do everything for everybody in every situation. Do what you can, and do it with a joyful heart.

5. Worry, frustration, anger, and procrastination will make you weary. Real, honest effort, on the contrary, will energize you. Act accordingly.

6. Keep going. One step at a time. True purpose has no time limit. True purpose has no deadline. Focus on the step you're taking.

7. No matter what, you can always fight the battles of just today. It's only when you add the infinite battles of yesterday and tomorrow that life gets overly complicated.

Once you replace busyness with mindfulness, you'll find the path opens wider for you to accomplish the priorities that are most important to you.

CHAPTER 3

Letting Go: Surrender Attachments That Are Holding You Back

Accept what is, let go of what was, and have faith in your journey.

"Yesterday afternoon my twin sister called me from her hospital room. She'd been in a coma for almost a year now. We actually spent the entire night together, talking and laughing. She's still weak, of course, but entering the holiday season and New Year with my sister back at my side is a priceless feeling."

That was the opening paragraph of an email we received last December from a reader named Amber. It caught our attention for obvious reasons.

Amber went on to say, "But you know what the really crazy thing is? A month before my sister's accident, we got in a ridiculous argument and didn't speak to each other for that entire month. And today, honestly, neither one of us can even remember why we were so darn mad. I'm so grateful we were able to let it go and get

another chance to love each other. We were just being stubborn
and holding on to the wrong thoughts."

Wow! Talk about a wake-up call, and a great reminder for all
of us to *let it go*. Letting go is about eliminating your attachments
and expectations about how things "have to be" in order to be
good enough right now, which clears space in your life to create an
even better tomorrow. Often we hold on to an idea of what *should*
have happened or what *should* be. We let the weight of these
thoughts sit heavily on our shoulders and interfere with our ability
to take our best step forward today. But this is, in a sense, holding
on to something that is not reality. It's holding on to an expectation
of how we think life should have been, because we want to control
the narrative.

We know how difficult it can be to let go of ideas of what we
think *should be* and instead focus on what *is* and what we can do
about it. As we shared in the introduction, one of our best friends
died unexpectedly when we were in our late twenties, and then
shortly thereafter Angel's brother died by suicide. In the months
that followed, Angel saw how her grief allowed her to pay attention
to, and understand the power of, the act of letting go. Wading
through the grief and the mourning, Angel was at first simply
unable to face the reality of the situation. Losing both of these
people in such a short time was incredibly difficult, and it took
months to gather herself and truly recognize what had happened.

It wasn't until she took a step back to appreciate all the time she
did get to spend with them, to recognize the great memories and
the fortune of having known them, that she was able to let go
of thinking that their deaths should not have happened. She realized
that their being gone was something she couldn't control, and that
thinking she could control it was an idea that would pull her under

if she kept clinging to it. But once she let go of wishing she could somehow bring them back, she was able to find ways to honor the memories of her brother and our friend and help them live on.

Ultimately, we grew to appreciate that although death is an ending, it is also a necessary part of living. And even though endings like these often seem ugly, they are necessary for beauty too—otherwise, it's impossible to appreciate someone or something, because they are unlimited. Limits illuminate beauty, and death is the ultimate limit—a reminder that we need to be aware of this beautiful person, and appreciate this beautiful thing called life. Death is also a beginning, because while we have lost someone special, this ending, like the loss of any wonderful life situation, is a moment of reinvention. Although deeply sad, their passing forces us to reinvent our lives, and in this reinvention is an opportunity to experience beauty in new, unseen ways and places. And finally, death is an opportunity to celebrate a person's life, and to be grateful for the beauty they showed us.

As human beings, we sometimes get used to the weight of grief and how it holds us in place. For instance, Angel often tells people, "My brother will die over and over again for the rest of my life, and I'm okay with that—it keeps me closer to him." This was Angel's way of reminding us that grief doesn't disappear, even when we let a person go. Step-by-step, breath by breath, it becomes a part of us. And it can become a healthy part of us too. Although we may never completely stop grieving, simply because we never stop loving the ones we've lost, we can lean on our love for them in the present. We can love them and emulate them by living with their magnificence as our daily inspiration.

We've also seen the power of letting go when it comes to relationships that no longer fit where we are in our lives—people who, for whatever reason, no longer match up with our goals and dreams for ourselves. Not too long ago, we gradually came to see how one of our childhood friends—we'll call him John—had started to become a toxic presence in our lives. Marc and John had been friends since grade school until Marc finally told him, "Enough is enough!" Although the two of them had grown up together, they had ended up on different planets when it came to their core life values. John believed there was one right way to do things—go to college, get a degree, get a job, and dedicate every waking moment of your life to climbing the corporate ladder. Marc, though, had other plans.

Although Marc did get a degree and a good job after college, in our free time as a couple, amid our ongoing struggle to cope with loss, we had also started writing articles on our blog, *Marc & Angel Hack Life*. But as the blog's reach grew, we encountered John discrediting our success on a daily basis. Whenever Marc shared one of our small success stories, John would say something negative like "Whatever. It's just a blog. I have one too."

Then when we quit our jobs to work on the blog full time, John basically told Marc we'd fail. "That's ridiculous! You had good jobs," John said. "You're just playing with fire in this economy, if you ask me." To which Marc eventually replied, "I'm not asking you!" That was the beginning of the end of Marc and John's friendship. Years later, their relationship is now a mere shadow of what it once was—and our life is honestly far brighter for it. Letting this friend go wasn't easy for Marc, but it was necessary for his own well-being and growth.

It's sad but true: no matter what you do or how much you explain yourself, some people will gradually evolve away from the things you value in life and the type of person you want to be. As time goes on, they will prove over and over again that they are no longer aligned with your values and needs. You are the average of the five people you spend the most time with. So be willing to release, or at least temporarily distance yourself from, the relationships or opinions that aren't helping you become the best version of yourself.

Signs It's Time to Let Go

Whether you're dealing with the loss of a loved one, a toxic relationship, a bad habit, or something else that's not serving your needs, it's not always easy to know when to let go. Most of the time, it's tough to be honest about what we really need and how our lives might benefit by letting go of some things. If you've felt any of the following, maybe it's time to reassess your situation.

Someone Constantly Expects You to Be Someone You're Not

A great relationship is about two things: first, appreciating the similarities, and second, respecting the differences. So be cordial, but don't completely change who you are for someone else simply because it's what *they* want, or because it's what *they* think is best for you.

If someone expects you to be someone you're not, take a step back. It's wiser to lose relationships over being who you are than to keep them intact by pretending to be someone else. It's easier to nurse a little heartache and meet someone new than it is to piece together your own shattered identity. It's easier to fill an empty space in your life where somebody else used to be than to fill the empty space within yourself where *you* used to be.

A Person's Actions Don't Match Their Words

Be wary of people who only tell you what you want to hear. It's so easy to believe someone when they're telling you exactly what you want to hear, but you have to watch what they do too. Actions speak louder than words; they speak the whole truth.

Everybody deserves somebody who helps them look forward to tomorrow. If someone has the opposite effect on you, because they are consistently inconsistent and their actions never match up with their words, it might be time to let them go. It's always better to be alone than to be in bad company. In the end, true friendship is a promise made in the heart—silent, unwritten, unbreakable by distance, and unchangeable by time. So don't just listen to what your friends say; watch what they do over the long term. Your true friends will slowly reveal themselves.

You Have a Habit of Moping and Feeling Sorry for Yourself

If you don't like something, change it. If you can't change it, change the way you think about it. Being hurt is something you can't control, but being miserable is always your choice. No matter how bad things are, you can always make them worse. Negative thinking creates negative results. Positive thinking creates positive results. Period. The only limits to the possibilities in your life tomorrow are the "buts" you use today.

> If you don't like something, change it.

Eventually you will realize that happiness is not the absence of problems, but simply the ability to deal with them well. Imagine all the wondrous things your mind might embrace if it weren't wrapped so tightly around your struggles. Always look at what you have instead of what you have lost. Because it's not what the world takes away from you that counts, it's what you do with what you have left.

You're Clutching Tight to an Easy-Street Mentality

Great accomplishments aren't easy, but they're worth it! So forget how you feel and remember what you deserve. Right *now* is always the best time to break out of your shell. You must take chances, make mistakes, and learn the lessons along the way.

Big challenges often prepare us for extraordinary success. Every struggle presents us with an experience or a lesson. A great journey is never easy, and no dose of adversity along the way is ever a waste of time if we learn and grow from it.

Remember, an arrow can only be shot by pulling it backward. When life pulls you back with difficulties, it means it's eventually going to launch you forward in a positive direction, as long as you keep your focus. So keep focusing, and keep aiming!

You Truly Dislike Your Current Situation

In life, it's always better to be at the bottom of the ladder you want to climb rather than the top of the one you don't. So don't let people who gave up on their goals talk you out of going after yours. The best thing you can do in most situations is to follow your intuition. Take risks. Don't just make the safe, easy choices because you're afraid of what might happen. If you do, nothing good will ever happen.

It's not always about trying to fix something that's broken.

Sometimes it's about starting over and creating something new. Sometimes you need to distance yourself to see things clearly. Sometimes growing stronger means growing apart from old habits, relationships, and circumstances, and finding something different that truly moves you—something that gets you so excited you can't wait to get out of bed in the morning. That's what *living* is all about. Don't just settle for the default settings in life, when you can customize it instead.

Your goals and needs can change, and that's okay. What was right for you once isn't necessarily right for you now. Sometimes the hardest part of letting go is realizing that you've changed, and then learning to start over with your new truth. If you find you're no longer learning anything new, it may be time to let some things go.

You Catch Yourself Obsessing Over and Living In the Past

Grasping on to what's no longer there holds too many of us back. We spend the vast majority of our lives recounting the past and letting it steer the course of the present. If all you do is attempt to relive something that's already happened, you're missing out. Don't waste your time trying to live in another time and place. Let it go! You must accept the end of something in order to build something new. So close some old doors today. Not because of pride, inability, or egotism, but simply because you've entered each of them already and realized that they led nowhere.

For example, carrying the weight of anger, resentment, and hatred over past events will not only hold you back, but also block your present blessings and opportunities. Even after the toughest times, eventually you will overcome the heartache and forget the reasons you cried and who caused the pain. You will realize that the secret to happiness and freedom is not about control or revenge, but about letting things unfold naturally and learning from your experiences over time. And you learn this more quickly when you consciously let go.

The mental space you create by releasing things that are already behind you gives you the chance to fill the space with something fresh and valuable. So let go of the past, set yourself free, and open your mind to the possibility of a new beginning.

Above all, remember that "human" is the only real label we are born with. Too often we forget this simple fact. To become attached to an opinionated label of depressed, divorced, diseased, rejected, or poor is to be like the rain, which doesn't know it is also the clouds, or the ice, which forgets it is water. For we are far more than the shape we're currently in. And we—like the wind, water, and sky—will change forms many times in our lives, while continuing to become our authentic selves.

How to Let Go and Move On

There's a quote that we often think of when we're considering how we'd like to control all aspects of our lives: "If you want to control the animals, give them a bigger pasture." If you have a pasture full of animals and they're all acting rowdy, can you really expect yourself to be able to control them?

No.

What you *can* do is give them a larger pasture. Let them roam. Let them graze and wander. By giving them some extra space, you'll see that relinquishing control can be freeing, and can even give you a new perspective on what's really important.

This same philosophy holds true for many aspects of life—stepping back and allowing certain things to happen means these things will take care of themselves *and* your needs will also be met. You will have less stress (and less to do) and more time and energy to work on the things that truly matter—the things you actually can control, like your attitude about everything.

This form of letting go is not giving up. It's about surrendering any obsessive attachments to specific people, outcomes, and situations. It means showing up every day in your life with the intention to be your best self, without expecting life to go a certain way. Have goals and dreams, take purposeful action, and build great relationships, but detach from what you think every aspect of your life "must" look like.

A big part of this type of liberating surrender is the daily practice of simply being a witness to the thoughts that are troubling you. Over the past decade, as we have worked with thousands of individuals, we've come to understand that the root cause of most human stress is our stubborn propensity to cling to stressful thoughts. In a nutshell, we hold on tight to the hope that things will go exactly as we imagine, and then we complicate our lives to no end when our imagination doesn't represent reality.

So how can we let go and live better? By realizing that there's nothing to hold on to in the first place. Most of the things—situations, problems, worries, ideals, expectations, etc.—we desperately try to grasp, as if they're real, solid, everlasting fixtures in our lives, aren't really there. Or if they are there in some form, they're changing, fluid, impermanent, or mostly created in our minds.

Life gets significantly easier to deal with when we understand this.

Imagine you're blindfolded and treading water in the center of a large swimming pool, and you're struggling desperately to grab the edge of the pool that you think is nearby, but it's really not—it's far away. Trying to grab that imaginary edge is stressing you out and tiring you as you splash around aimlessly, reaching to find and grab something that isn't there.

Now imagine you pause, take a deep breath, and realize that there's nothing nearby to hold on to—just water around you. You can continue to struggle with grasping at something that doesn't exist, or you can accept that there's only water around you and relax and float.

This is the art of letting go. And it starts with your thinking.

Being a Witness

Just because the world around you is confusing and chaotic doesn't mean the world within you has to be too. You can eliminate the confusion and chaos inside you created by others, the past, uncontrollable events, or your general frame of mind, by being a simple witness to your thoughts. It's about simply noticing at first, not interfering and not even judging, because by judging too rapidly you'll have lost the pure witness. The moment you rush to say, "This is good," or "This is bad," you'll have already grabbed hold of the chaos.

It takes a little time to create a gap between the witnessing of thoughts and your reaction to them. Once the gap is there, though, you are in for a great surprise—you discover that you are not the thoughts themselves, or the chaos influencing them. You are merely an observer, one who's capable of letting go, changing your mind, and rising above the turmoil.

This process of thought watching is the very alchemy of the

"mindfulness" we discussed in chapter 2. Because as you become more and more deeply rooted in watching and witnessing, the confusing, chaotic thoughts start disappearing. You are thinking, but the mind is empty of senseless chatter. You are floating, with no extra weight and a lot less effort. It's a moment of enlightenment—a moment that you become, perhaps for the first time, an unconditioned and truly free human being.

So today, let this be your reminder to release all the small annoyances. Move through your day consciously. Try to notice at least one insignificant frustration that you would normally get worked up about. Then do yourself a favor and simply let it go. Experience, in this little way, the freedom of being in control of the way you feel. And realize that you can extend this same level of control to every situation you encounter in life.

At almost any given moment, the way you feel is the way you *choose* to feel, and the way you react is the way you choose to react. When you let go, you think better, and you live better. Instead of attempting to fit your thoughts and concerns into the small space in which you believe they belong, do your best to release them. And yes, you can do this even if the past is painful. Holding on is like believing that there's only a past; letting go and moving forward is knowing in your heart that there's a bright future ahead.

One of our readers, Evan, was experiencing a related situation recently; he was struggling with letting go of a failed relationship, and the negativity of that relationship was crippling his thinking and leaking into his everyday life. In an email to us, Evan explained the signs and symptoms of this toxic relationship, one that had been heading south for many years. He admitted that he needed to let go, but he struggled to do so because it meant finally facing reality, which would require him to release the beliefs he had had about how his life and relationship were supposed to turn out. One line from his email summed it up well: *"I'm learning the hard way that the hardest thing in life is simply letting go of what you thought was real."*

As Evan pointed out, letting go and moving on is difficult. It involves facing the fears and disappointments of the past that are binding your spirit, and this process can be scary. You need to learn to accept this fear, so you can start to move past it. If you feel like you need to let something go, but you simply haven't been able to do so, know that you're not alone. Accepting what is, letting go, and moving on are skills that all of us must learn when facing the realities of life, but they take time to master.

Here are some additional strategies and perspectives for making this happen:

Accept the truth and be thankful. To let go is to be thankful for the experiences that made you laugh, made you cry, and helped you learn and grow. It's the acceptance of everything you have, everything you once had, and the possibilities that lie ahead. It's all about finding the strength to embrace life's changes, with gratitude.

Distance yourself for a while. Sometimes you need to take a few steps back to gain clarity about a situation. The best way to do this is to simply take a break and explore something else for a while. Then you can return to where you started and see things with a new perspective. And the people there may see you differently too. Returning to where you started is entirely different from never leaving.

Focus only on what can be changed. Realize that not everything in life is meant to be modified or perfectly understood. Live, let go, learn what you can, and don't waste energy worrying about the things you can't change. Focus exclusively on what you can change, and if you can't change something you don't like, change the way you think about it. Review your options, and then reframe what you don't like into a starting point for achieving something better.

Claim ownership and full control of your life. No one else is responsible for you. You are in full control of your being. Throughout life, you may have learned that you should blame your parents, your teachers, your mentors, the education system, the government, etc., but never yourself. Right? It's never, ever your fault. *Wrong!* It's always your fault, because if you want to change, if you want to let go and move on with your life, you're the only person who can make it happen.

Focus inward. Yes, it's important to help others, but you have to start with yourself. If you're looking outside yourself to find where you fit in or how you can create an impact, look inside yourself instead. Review who you already are, the lifestyle you're currently living, and what makes you feel alive. Then nurture these things and make positive adjustments until your present life can no longer contain them, forcing you to grow and move beyond your existing circumstances.

Find a new crowd. Some people come into your life just to strengthen you so you can move on without them. They are supposed to be part of your memory, not your destiny. When you have to start compromising your happiness and your potential for the people around you, it's time to change who you spend your time with. It's time to join local meet-ups, attend conferences, network online, and find a more supportive tribe.

Take a chance. When life sets you up with a challenge, there's a reason for it; it's meant to test your courage and willingness to make a change and take a chance on something new. Life only moves in one direction: forward. This challenge is your chance to let go of the old and make way for the new. Your destiny awaits your decision.

Focus on today. You can decide right now that negative experiences from your past will not predict your future. Figure out what the next positive step is, no matter how small or difficult, and take it. Take one step forward without hesitation, without looking back.

Forgive with all your heart, as often as necessary. Forgiveness is a constant attitude of choosing happiness over hurt and acceptance over resistance. It's about acknowledging that we're all mistaken sometimes; even the best of us do foolish things on occasion that can have severe consequences. But it doesn't mean we are evil and unforgivable, or that we can't ever be trusted again. Know this. Sit with it. It might take time to forgive, because it takes strength to forgive. Because when you forgive, you love with all your might. This forgiveness—true forgiveness—brings you to where you can sincerely say, "Thank you for that experience."

Embrace your quirks, your mistakes, and the fact that life is a lesson. Life is a ride. Things change, people change, but you will always be *you*; so stay true to yourself and never sacrifice who you are for anyone or anything. You have to dare to be yourself, in this moment, however frightening or strange that self may prove to be. It's about realizing that even on your weakest days, you still get a little bit stronger, if you're willing to learn. This is why sometimes the greatest thing to come out of all your trouble and hard work isn't what you get, but who you become.

Nurture your self-worth. Sometimes the hardest part of the journey is simply believing you're worthy of the trip. And you are! So watch your mind and stop any self-deprecating thoughts. Remind yourself that once upon a time, in an unguarded, honest moment, you recognized yourself as a worthy friend. The world starts to respond when you believe that about yourself. It doesn't always look like you thought it would, but positive shifts begin when you start to recognize and acknowledge your own self-worth.

Do everything with a touch of kindness. In tough situations, three things are vitally important: the first is to be kind; the second is to be kind; and the third is—you guessed it—to be kind. Whatever you do can be done more effectively when you add kindness. Whatever words you speak will always be more compelling when expressed with kindness. The kind deeds you perform in just one moment can have a positive impact that lasts a lifetime. Your days will be brighter and your years fuller when you add kindness to your purpose. Choose to be kind every day, and you'll truly be choosing to live in a world with less stress and more happiness.

Finally, it's crucial to remind yourself repeatedly that letting go is *not* giving up. Letting go is surrendering any unhealthy attachment to specific people, outcomes, and situations. It means showing up every day in your life with the intention to be your best self, and to do the best you know how, without expecting things to go a certain way.

> Letting go is *not* giving up.

Fifteen Things to Let Go Of

Letting go is undoubtedly a challenge we all face, in one way or another, every day of our lives. That's why we've listed fifteen things—little, healthy reminders—to help you kick-start the process. You'll be amazed at how good you'll feel after you take some of these toxic elements out of your life. Start by letting go of:

1. **Your temper.** Never do something permanently foolish just because you are temporarily upset.
2. **Petty grudges.** Life is far too short to be spent nursing bitterness and registering wrongs. If there's someone in your life who deserves another chance, give it to them. If you need to apologize, do it. Give your story together a happy, new beginning.
3. **Lingering false beliefs.** Stop from time to time and ask yourself, "Is this true?" It's funny how we can sometimes manipulate things and fit them into our version of reality. But thinking something does not make it true. Wanting something does not make it real. So watch your thoughts. Be wise. When your identity is not rooted in the truth, it

leads to a distorted version of reality—a self-created world.

4. **Yesterday's tragedies.** You are not what has happened to you; you are what you choose to become in this moment. Drop the needless burden, take a deep breath, and start again. Ultimately, you will know you are on the right track in life when you become uninterested in looking back and eager to take the next step.

5. **Life's small annoyances.** Don't let dumb little things break your happiness. Frustration and stress come from the way you react, not the way things are. Adjust your attitude, and the frustration and stress will be gone.

6. **The idea that some people are below you.** Even if you've worked really hard to get to where you are in life, there's no such thing as a self-made person. Someone believed in, encouraged, and invested in you. Be grateful, and be that someone for others too. No one ever made themselves strong in the long run by showing how small someone else is. So don't make lazy assumptions about people. Ask about their ideas and stories. Then listen. Be patient. Be willing to learn. Be kind. Be a good neighbor.

7. **The belief that material possessions make you who you are.** You are not defined by what you have physically acquired in this world. Remember to remain humble. Ultimately, two things define you more than anything else: your patience when you have very little, and your mindset when you have more than enough.

8. **Seeking happiness outside yourself.** You have to create your own sunshine. True happiness starts from within. Read

something positive every morning, and do something positive before you go to sleep at night. Keep your focus on all the positive possibilities and opportunities, and you will feel great. Feel great, and you will do great things.

9. **Wanting to be repaid for every good deed you do.** Don't worry too much about what's in it for you every single second. If you're making a positive contribution to others, there's always something in it for you. You were born with the ability to change someone's life. Don't ever waste it. Be giving. Be present. Be someone who makes a difference.

10. **All the little white lies and charades.** How do you build credibility? It's simple: be honest. Follow through. Honor your promises. Apologize when you screw up. Be the type of person you'd want to meet and spend time with. The type of person whose actions, words, and values are always in agreement.

11. **Fearing what your intuition is telling you to do.** Fear kills more dreams than failure ever will. So don't let fear shut you down; let it wake you up. Do one thing every day that scares you. The more you act on your intuition fearlessly, the more your intuition will serve you. If you genuinely feel something, pay attention.

12. **Waiting for the stars to align.** Remember, you don't always need the perfect plan. Sometimes you just need to give it a try, let go, and see what happens. To paraphrase Maya Angelou: Just do the best you can until you know better. Then once you know better, do better.

13. **An "all or nothing" view of success.** Appreciate the gray area between the extremes of success and failure—the journey, the process, the path—what you're learning, how you're helping others learn too, and the growing process you allow yourself to participate in. And above all, never let success get to your head or failure get to your heart.

14. **Self-criticism.** No one is inspired by your misery or self-deprecating comments. Let go of thinking that giving up the wrong things means failure. Giving up and moving on are two very different things. If you wish to inspire yourself and others, be joyful. Have fun. Love yourself. Forgive yourself. Accept yourself. Be unapologetically *you*.

15. **Changing just to impress people.** Change because it makes you a better person and leads you to a brighter future. Change because you know it's the right thing to do for *you*. Not everyone needs to like you, and some people won't, no matter what you do. Try not to take the things these people say about you personally. What they think and say is a reflection on them, not you.

It's always necessary to accept when some part of your life has reached its inevitable end. The secret to getting ahead is to focus your energy not on fixing and fighting the old, but on building and growing something new. *Closing the door, completing the chapter, turning the page*—whatever you call it, what matters is that you find the strength to leave in the past those parts of your life that are over. Start by identifying and letting go of just one or two of the things in the list above, and you'll begin to accrue the rewards of accepting reality for what it is.

What You Learn as You Let Go of the Uncontrollable

Letting go is *not* easy, and it's a journey that is traveled one day at a time. But if you stick with it, you will ultimately learn some valuable life lessons. You'll learn that stepping onto a new path is difficult, but no more difficult than remaining in a situation that no longer fits or no longer exists. You'll learn that letting go doesn't mean you don't care about something or someone anymore; it's just realizing that the only thing you really have control over in this moment is yourself. And you'll learn that in order to be free, to get back to happy, you must let go of the need for certainty.

Remember, the opposite of certainty is not uncertainty; it's openness, curiosity, and a willingness to embrace life as it is rather than resisting it. We're no strangers to making way for new chapters in our lives, and we understand the discomfort that comes from change. We've endured loss, struggled through unemployment, dealt with painful failures and toxic relationships, and become new parents. But we've also seen the life-changing benefits of letting go of situations, ideas, people, and habits that are holding us back.

Marc is relearning this lesson now:

> *This morning I met up with an old friend, someone whom I care about deeply but have internally struggled with for years because I've always been worried about her health.*
>
> *I want to help her heal, because I feel I'm losing her.*

I want to teach her the time-tested tools for living a happier, simpler, healthier life that I've helped so many other people with, so she can give up her unhealthy habits, take up exercise and mindfulness, nurture her needs, and be transformed into a healthy person again.

But that's not reality. I want to control something that frightens me, but I can't do anything about it. Because I'm not in control of anyone but myself. I want to help my friend, but she's not interested in being helped. She's actually told me so a dozen times in the past.

So today, I let go.

Not "let go" as in "let her go." I "let go" as in I stopped trying to control and change her, and instead took a deep breath and accepted her for exactly who she is.

And guess what? I discovered that who she is is a blessing. Who she is is someone so ridiculously special and unique I have a hard time expressing it. She's hilarious and passionate and compassionate and wise and wild and thoughtful and loyal—and did I mention wild?

When I let go and accepted her whole truth, only then could I actually enjoy all of her, *instead of worrying about losing her or changing her ways.*

And this, I've learned, is the best way to be in most areas of life. As long as a person isn't in immediate danger, or causing someone else to be in danger, you can stop trying to change them. You can just let go and dissolve into their presence, notice who they really are, appreciate every quirk. You can stop complaining about

Just be. Just accept. Just appreciate.

your life circumstances and your losses, and about how the world is, and just let go and love what is. Just be. Just accept. Just appreciate.

Just breathe.

As you read these words, you are breathing. Stop for a moment and notice this breath. You can control this breath and make it faster or slower, or make it behave as you like. Or you can simply let yourself inhale and exhale naturally.

There is peace in just letting your lungs breathe, without having to control the situation or do anything about it. Now imagine letting other parts of your body breathe, like your tense shoulders. Just let them be, without having to tense them or control them.

Now look around the room you're in and notice the objects around you. Pick one, and let it breathe. There are likely people in the room with you too, or in the same house or building, or in nearby houses or buildings. Visualize them in your mind, and let them breathe.

When you let everything and everyone breathe, you just let them be, exactly as they are. You don't need to control them, worry about them, or change them. You just let them breathe, in peace, and you accept them as they are. This is what letting go of the uncontrollable is all about. It can be a life-changing practice.

The bottom line is that things will happen that are unexpected, undesirable, and uncontrollable. You can choose to hold on to the things you can't control. But if you want to get back to happy, you have to be willing to release some of those things. You can't control everything that happens to you, or everything that happens around you. All you *can* control is your response. The closing exercise below gives you a chance to look at the ways you're framing the narrative of your life and understand how to step back, let go, and move forward.

Closing Exercise

Many of the biggest misunderstandings in life could be avoided if we simply took the time to ask, "What else could this mean?" A wonderful way to do this is by using a reframing tool we initially picked up from research professor Brené Brown, which we then tailored through our coaching work with students and clients. We call the tool *The story I'm telling myself.* Although asking the question itself—"What else could this mean?"—can help reframe our thoughts and broaden our perspectives, using the simple phrase *The story I'm telling myself* as a prefix to troubling thoughts has undoubtedly created many "aha moments" for our students and clients in recent times.

Here's how it works: *The story I'm telling myself* can be applied to any difficult life situation or circumstance in which a troubling thought is getting the best of you. For example, perhaps someone you love (husband, wife, boyfriend, girlfriend, etc.) didn't call you on their lunch break when they said they would, and now an hour has passed and you're feeling upset because you're obviously not a high enough priority to them. When you catch yourself feeling this way, use the phrase: *The story I'm telling myself is that they didn't call me because I'm not a high enough priority to them.*

Then ask yourself these questions:

- Can I be absolutely certain this story is true?
- How do I feel and behave when I tell myself this story?
- What's one other possibility that might also make the ending to this story true?

Give yourself the space to think it all through carefully. Challenge yourself to think differently! *The story I'm telling myself* and the three related questions give you tools for revisiting and reframing the troubling or confusing situations that arise in your daily life. From there, you can challenge the stories you subconsciously tell yourself and do a reality check with a more objective mindset. This will ultimately allow you to let go of the stories that aren't helping you get back to happy, and make better decisions about every aspect of your life.

CHAPTER 4

Self-Love: Commit to Putting Yourself on Your To-Do List

The most powerful relationship you will ever have is your relationship with yourself.

When we were starting out in business, we had it all wrong, focusing too much on how others perceived us, overcommitting to everything, and getting beaten down by overwhelming amounts of self-inflicted stress and negativity. There was no room for loving ourselves. It wasn't even on our radars. We both experienced this in very real ways. And then Angel experienced it all over again after the birth of our son:

After Mac was born, I was trying to do it all. I was trying to be the best mother, the best wife, the best housekeeper, the best chef. I was taking responsibility for everything. The thought going through my mind was I can't do this; I'm not good enough. I would totally break down. It was too much for me to handle, but I didn't want to recognize that; I didn't want to speak those words out loud. After a couple months of parenthood, I finally was able to start making time to be with myself, to breathe, to not let the weight of my responsibility of being a mom and wife overtake me.

It took time, but I learned to sit quietly, love myself, and be proud of the progress I'd made as a mother and in the family that I was building. As a result, I was much happier. I wasn't badgering myself all the time, telling myself I wasn't good enough. Once I started focusing more on self-love, I was able to be more present and accept that I have great qualities to offer and I am good enough. I know that I'm constantly improving and learning to be okay with who I am in the moment.

Eventually, through these types of experiences, we both learned that if we can't gain the capacity for self-love—to open our hearts and minds to our own needs—we won't grow, and we won't ever have the capacity to fully love each another. We learned that when there is love inside us, there is life inside us.

Defining Self-Love

Self-love is learning to create space for yourself; it's putting yourself on your to-do list, scheduling time and space to practice spiritual and healthy living, both physically and mentally. Self-love is making sure that our lives aren't constant busyness, rushing, and obligation. Rather, it's managing our time wisely enough to know that we need to get enough rest, feed our passions, and support ourselves in every way we need to.

When self-love is present, you can take risks and experience curiosity, astonishment, sudden joy, and all the other occurrences that reveal the beauty of your growing spirit. And even if things don't turn out as planned, you'll still have a foundation of love and acceptance within you to fall back on.

It's not always easy to embrace self-love. We know that. One of the greatest struggles in life is the struggle to accept, embrace, and love ourselves, with all of our imperfections; to be honest about who we are, how we feel, and what we need; to stop discrediting ourselves for everything we aren't and start giving ourselves credit for everything we are; and finally, to be aware that not everyone we love will agree with us every step of the way and to be okay with that.

If you're low on self-love, you're never going to feel like you're doing enough for the people you love, the businesses you run, the employers who provide your livelihood. We have to learn to be our own best friends, because sometimes we fall too easily into the trap of being our own worst enemies. We fall in love with the idea of others loving us, and we forget to love ourselves.

You are truly worth loving.

Despite your past self-neglect, you are truly worth loving. You just need to find that truth in yourself and say *yes*. The discovery process begins now.

Turning from Self-Neglect to Self-Love

Everyone experiences unhappy circumstances on occasion, but there's a big difference between having bouts of unhappiness and living a habitually unhappy life. Although there are some exceptions (such as clinical depression), in our coaching experience the vast majority of people's unhappiness stems in large part from self-neglect.

Even if you are generally a happy person, neglecting yourself is a habit—or ritual—that can easily creep up on you. The key is to give yourself the extra attention you need and deserve. Resisting and ignoring your own feelings does not serve you. It leads to stress, illness, confusion, broken relationships, anger, and depression. If you have experienced any of the above, you know that these states of mind can be horrifically unhealthy; when you're in the habit of self-neglect, your standards for living nose-dive, and it becomes harder and harder to escape.

Right now, ask yourself: "Do I love myself enough to never lower my standards for the wrong reasons?" Find the strength to say *yes*!

Life is about living honorably. It's about doing the right thing for *you*, no matter what, even when nobody else knows or understands. At the end of the day, your reputation is what other people know about you. Your honor is what you know about yourself.

You have to admit, you've spent a lot of your life subconsciously belittling yourself. Thinking you're not enough. Trying to be someone else. Someone who fits in, who's less sensitive, needy, and flawed. Someone who is less *you*. Because you felt broken and didn't want to scare people away. You wanted to make a good impression and have people like you. To be seen as worthy and loveable so you could feel healed and whole. And for the longest time, behind a facade of fake smiles, you have inadvertently betrayed yourself for the purpose of pleasing everyone else. And for the longest time, your heart has ached.

But now you're seeing things differently. Belittling yourself just doesn't make sense anymore. And more than that, you now realize no matter what you do or how you change, some people will never like you anyway.

You now realize you have to start doing things for the right reasons.

Not because it's what you think everyone else needs, but

because you finally know yourself to be worthy of your own love and care.

Not because other people approve of you, but because you are breathing your own air, thinking your own thoughts, and occupying a space no one else ever could.

You may have been beaten down by adversity, or sidetracked by rejection, but you are not broken. So don't let others convince you otherwise. Heal yourself by refusing to belittle yourself. Choose to stand out, to do what you know in your heart is right. Choose to appreciate yourself for who you are, accepting your quirks entirely and sincerely. Make self-love a daily ritual. When you choose to shift from self-loathing to self-love like this, you'll find profound healing and growth in every area of your life. Whenever we see happy, successful people, we smile, knowing that their lives are products of a series of decisions that directly support their love for themselves.

Remember that every second you spend doubting your worth and criticizing yourself is a tragic loss—a fresh moment of your life thrown away. Don't waste any more of your seconds. Today is the best day to start loving yourself.

How You Treat Yourself Emotionally

We can be our own harshest critics. Our minds become battle-grounds of self-hate, making it almost impossible to make room for positivity, acceptance, and self-love. *Almost* impossible. But you can crack open that possibility if you are willing. That's why addressing your emotional well-being is the first important focal point in the journey to reclaim and grow your self-love. One way we love to do this is by attending to ourselves through meditation.

And you can start to gain emotional well-being in as little as five minutes at the very beginning of your day. Right after you wake up, start by noticing the sounds around you and the way your body feels. Do a quick body scan, starting at your feet, then moving up into your shins and into your knees and your quads, and so on. What does it feel like to be in your body for these few minutes? Look around the room at the sunlight reflected on the wall, or light a candle and pay attention to the flicker of its flame.

Spending a few minutes noticing like this can help you begin your day in a centered place. We started this practice when we realized we were jumping up out of bed each day and checking our smartphones before we'd even kissed each other good morning. We learned that by starting the day in a hectic frame of mind, that anxiety trickled into the next thing, and the next. Our day was in complete chaos. We were the opposite of presence. Each hectic morning felt like it was wasted, because it didn't start with presence. It didn't start with peace. But instituting a simple morning meditation practice like the one above can set the tone for the rest of the day and make a world of difference.

When we think we aren't worth anything, it negatively affects every other aspect of our lives. But when we treat ourselves well mentally, the world around us becomes brighter. So how do we do that? Let's look at some specific ways to treat ourselves better mentally.

Practicing Self-Inquiry Through Journaling

We use the process of self-inquiry a lot with our students. It's based in Buddhist and Eastern philosophy and adapted from the teachings of Alan Watts and Byron Katie. It is a practice of asking yourself a series of simple but revealing questions. This self-care process in practice has improved our lives drastically. It's an exercise for times when something's getting the better of you and you're not feeling so great about yourself.

When a troubling thought is going through your head, write it down. Then go back a day or two later, when you're feeling calm and collected, and try to look at that thought more objectively, from a place of love, presence, and open-mindedness. Ask yourself, "Is this true?" "Can this thought be proven?" "Who am I with this thought in my head?" "Who would I be, and what else would I see, if I were able to remove it? What is the complete opposite of this thought, and is there at least some truth in the opposite?" Repeat this practice of writing down your troubling thoughts daily. Then spend at least one day a week reviewing your thoughts and asking the self-inquiry questions.

After a few weeks, you'll start to see patterns. You'll start to realize that some of the same ideas are troubling you day in and day out. That awareness will help you catch yourself in the act. The next time a negative thought returns, along with the anxiety that typically comes with it, you'll be able to say to yourself, "I've seen this before and it's okay. It's okay that this thought is here." And you'll have a different story to tell yourself about that thought, one that might change your outlook for the better.

Tell Yourself You're Good Enough

This might seem overly simplistic, but it's vital: Tell yourself, "I am *enough!*" whenever you begin to feel like you aren't. Sometimes the hardest part of the journey is simply believing you're worthy of the trip. And you are! Accept your flaws. Admit your mistakes. Don't hide, and don't lie. Deal with your truth, and grow stronger from it. Your truth won't penalize you. You are always good enough just the way you are, and you can grow stronger than you ever have been before. The mistakes you make along the way won't hurt you, but the denial and cover-up will. Flawed people are beautiful, likeable, and teachable.

You are *you* for a reason. Ignore the distractions. Listen to your own inner voice. Mind your own business. Keep your best wishes and your biggest goals close to your heart and dedicate time to them every day. Don't be scared to walk alone, and don't be scared to love it. Don't let anyone's ignorance, drama, or negativity derail you from your truth and from loving who you are. And remember that rejections don't matter in the long run. Accept them and re-focus your attention on what *does* matter.

What does matter is how you see yourself. Make a habit of staying true to your values and convictions, regardless of what others think. Never be ashamed of doing what feels right. To help you implement this positive habit, start by making a list of a few things that are important to you when it comes to building your character and living your life. For example, you might include qualities such as honesty, reliability, self-respect, self-discipline, compassion, and kindness. Having a short list like this to refer to will give you an opportunity to consciously invoke and uphold your handpicked traits and behaviors instead of doing something else simply for external validation.

Believe You're Capable of Overcoming the Challenges You Face

Great challenges make life interesting; overcoming them makes life meaningful. Self-loving people know this and they live accordingly. The way you deal with life's challenges determines your level of success and happiness. So laugh at your mistakes and learn from them. Joke about your troubles and gather strength from them. Have fun with the challenges you face and then conquer them.

Will doing so always feel comfortable? Absolutely not. But will it be worth it? You betcha! Emotional discomfort in life, when accepted, rises, crests, and crashes in a series of waves. Each wave washes away an old layer of you and deposits treasures you never expected to find. Out goes inexperience, in comes awareness; out goes frustration, in comes resilience; out goes hatred, in comes kindness. No one would say these waves of emotional experience are easy to ride, but the rhythm of discomfort that you learn to tolerate is natural, helpful, and necessary. The discomfort eventually leaves you stronger and healthier than it found you.

Choose Responsibility over Blame

When something negative happens, self-loving people look for a way to take responsibility rather than searching for someone to point a finger at. They know that placing responsibility and blame elsewhere doesn't solve the problem—it only stirs anxiety and helplessness. By choosing to take full responsibility, you do yourself the favor of encouraging positive change and acceptance rather than stewing in sorrow and stagnation.

And keep in mind that taking responsibility doesn't mean that you dwell on the outcomes of the past; it means you own your decision in this moment and make the best of it.

Educate Yourself

As Mahatma Gandhi once said, "Live as if you were to die tomorrow. Learn as if you were to live forever." Life is a book, and those who do not educate themselves read only a few pages. When you know better, you live better and feel better about yourself. Self-loving people are keyed into this. And they know that *all* education is self-education. It doesn't matter if you're sitting in a college classroom or a coffee shop. We don't learn anything we don't want to learn. Those who take the time and initiative to pursue knowledge on their own are the only ones who earn a real education in this world.

Take a look at any widely acclaimed scholar, entrepreneur, artist, or historical figure. Whether they're formally educated or not, you'll find they are a product of continuous self-education, investing copious amounts of time and energy to improve themselves, which is one of the highest forms of self-love.

Feed Your Passions and Talents

If your life is going to mean anything, you have to live it yourself. You have to choose the path that feels right to *you*, not the one that looks right to everyone else. Each of us feels the gentle tug of fascination with some idea or activity. And sometimes that tug isn't so gentle. Self-loving people recognize and respect their inner longings as something important, and they devote their time and energy to nourishing those desires. They know that feeding their inner hunger is much more important than any fears they might have about what that might look like to others.

Our challenge to you is this: live your life in this world, on this day and every day thereafter, not as a bystander but as an active participant. Every morning, ask yourself what is really important to you, and then find the courage, wisdom, and willpower to build your day around your answer.

How You Treat Yourself Physically

It can be easy to forget to take care of your body and your physical health, especially if you're focused on tending to your mental self. But they are intrinsically linked, so the next time you're faced with the decision either to go for that walk or to skip it, remember that the benefit is not just for your physical body but for your mental health too.

One of our self-love practices is to go to the gym together five days a week. Every weekday morning around eight, we drop off Mac at child care, then head to the gym to get a good sweat going. We do this for our health, for our bodies—to feel strong, to feel beautiful. We also do it for the time together, to laugh with each other, share stories, and talk about whatever's on our minds while we're pumping iron and getting stronger.

If you treat your physical self well, your mind will also be exercised. And guess what? You don't have to exercise every day—there are many other ways to take care of your physical health. Here are a few more:

Manage Your Energy

Everything around you is made of energy, so pay attention to how you exchange energy in your life. To attract positive things into your being, start by sending out positive energy. Also consider how much energy it costs you to engage with certain activities and people. On the other side of the equation, notice how much energy you gain from other activities and people. Once you're feeling positive, remember that the secret to getting ahead is to focus all of your energy not on fixing and fighting the old, but on building and growing something new.

Take a Moment to Breathe

If you're feeling anxious or fearful, relax your mind and concentrate on your breath. Focus on increasing the length of each inhale and exhale. Inhale and count to six before you exhale; then exhale and count to six. Repeat this simple breathing exercise for one to two minutes, and it will connect you to your center and the present moment. Step away from the computer, from the conversation, from whatever is causing your immediate stress or anxiety. Keep calm and remember: the time to take a deep breath is when you think you don't have time for one.

Share the Load

Give up perfectionism and trying to do everything yourself. We know how easy it is to fall into the trap of thinking that if you want something done right, you have to do it yourself. But trust us when we say no one benefits—least of all you—when you run yourself ragged. Learn to delegate. If you can't afford to hire some help, find a way to barter. Discover the joy and reward of mentoring and training someone who may want to learn from you. Release your burden, and allow others to feel needed.

Commit to a Healthy Lifestyle

Exercise energizes you. We don't need to debate the physical benefits of exercise. Just do it. And don't skip meals when you are under pressure. If you do, you deprive your body and mind of the nutrients they need to perform at their best. When you eat, choose real food. Limit your intake of stimulants like caffeine and sugar. Doing so will help keep your energy stable throughout the day, avoiding the yo-yo of artificial morning highs followed by afternoon crashes.

Finally, don't sleep less to get more done. Sleep brings health, focus, and clarity.

Make Time to Connect with Others Face-to-Face

Life is more than text messages and tweets. Sometimes the message is lost in the medium. Online interactions can give us a false sense of connection, which is something we need to live a healthy and vibrant life. We all need human connection and physical touch, and nothing can replace the real-life physical interaction between two people that's great for both our physical and emotional health. Take digital breaks and spend more time connecting face-to-face with the people who matter to you.

Fuel the Machine First

Make time to eat breakfast every day. It really doesn't take that long. Place one half of a heaping cup of oatmeal and one cup of water in a microwave-safe bowl. Nuke it for two minutes. Add a dash of cinnamon, a handful of raisins, a handful of chopped walnuts, and a touch of maple syrup or honey.

Between meals choose an energy-boosting snack like a handful of almonds or a piece of fruit. Eat well to get energized.

In addition to the more tangible ways you can take care of yourself physically, there are some more subtle ways you can do this too.

Be Present and Engaged in the Only
Moment There Is: This One

Self-loving people value themselves, and therefore they value how they spend their time. They also realize that the only moment they ever truly have is the present moment, so they occupy it fully. Distractions are in the palms of our hands these days, but we need to remember to look up more often. Smile when you see people. Ask about their day. Listen.

You can't truly connect with anyone, including yourself, unless you're fully engaged. Detach from your device and reconnect yourself to the revitalizing energy that comes from actually experiencing real relationships and real life.

Do Something Every Day That Makes You Happy

There's a big difference between empty fatigue and gratifying exhaustion. Life is short, so invest in the activities that bring meaning into your life. A meaningful life is about making a decision every day to do something that moves you—caring for yourself by doing things you care about. It's a matter of realizing that there's nothing selfish about self-care. Because we can't give what we don't have.

> There's nothing selfish about self-care.

Make time to work toward accomplishing the personal priorities that move you closer to your life goals. Developing skills that move you forward in a positive direction will bring a wonderful sense of satisfaction to your life far beyond just being busy. You have to experience life on your terms before you can be helpful to others.

Mix Up a Stagnant Routine

Remember, the most important currency in life is experience. Money comes and goes, but your experiences stay with you until your last breath. So don't be afraid to mix things up and challenge yourself with new life experiences. Sometimes a break from your routine is the very thing you need. Just because you've always done it doesn't mean you have to continue. And just because you've never done it doesn't mean you can't start now.

Let Go of Needless Excess

When things aren't adding up in your life, start subtracting. Life gets easier when you delete the things and people that make it difficult. Get rid of some of life's complexities so you can spend more time with people you love and do more of the things you love. This means getting rid of the physical clutter and eliminating all but the essential, so you are left with only the things that give you value.

How You Let Others Treat You Emotionally

You may be wondering *How can I possibly control the way others treat me?* The truth is that you can't. Not completely. But don't worry. When you make yourself a priority and take care of yourself first, you become a better person for those in your life and you can begin to engage in relationships in more intentional and healthy ways.

Although you cannot truly control the way others treat you, there are countless ways you can control your own reactions to the circumstances that lead to more positive and emotionally enriching interactions with others.

Teach People How to Treat You

Not everyone will appreciate what you do for them. You have to figure out who's worth your attention and who's taking advantage of you. If your time and energy is being spent on the wrong relationships, you'll only end up in a tedious cycle of fleeting friendships and superficial romances that are as thrilling as they are meaningless, and wondering why you always seem to be chasing affection.

That's why self-loving people approach relationships from a place of self-respect and self-sufficiency. They don't expect everyone to like them, and they don't need everyone to. They know what they need to feel loved and respected, and they know what they have to offer others. Gently teach the people around you about your boundaries, and if they cross those boundaries repeatedly, have enough sense to take a step back.

Rein in Self-Deprecating Thoughts

If you feel like others aren't treating you with love and respect, check your price tag. Perhaps you've subconsciously marked yourself down. Self-loving people tell others what they're worth by showing them what they are willing to accept for their time and attention. So get off the clearance rack. If you don't value and respect yourself wholeheartedly, others won't either.

Distance Yourself from Those Who Bring You Down

Being in no relationship is better than being in a wrong one. Don't worry too much about folks who don't worry about you. Know your worth! When you give yourself to those who disrespect you, you lose. Your friends in life should motivate, inspire, and respect you. Your circle should be well rounded and supportive. Keep it tight. Quality over quantity, always.

Avoid Drama Circles

Don't get caught up in judging and gossiping. Don't give in to the negativity and drama around you. Be positive. Give people a piece of your heart rather than a piece of your mind. Life is too short to be spent talking about people and stirring up trouble that has no substance. Instead, get caught up in being thankful and kinder than necessary.

Be Aware of Social Conditioning

Knowing who you are is one thing, but truly believing in yourself and living as yourself is another. With all the social conditioning in our society, we sometimes forget to stay true to ourselves. Don't lose yourself out there. You can't attract the right people into your life when you're pretending to be someone else. So love yourself enough to be yourself, and if you can't find a group whose values and consciousness match your own, be the source of one. Others with similar values and consciousness will be drawn to you in turn.

Avoid Dishonesty and Insincerity

In life and business, our reputation is always more important than our next paycheck, and our integrity is worth more than our next thrill. A cheater's punishment is to live a life of mistrust and un-certainty. They live in constant fear that the people they cheated on will also cheat on them. And that's just the beginning of a downward spiral. When our identity is not rooted in honesty, it can lead to all kinds of dangerous and lonely places where we seek approval for the wrong reasons and from the wrong people. Don't live like this. Speak your truth. Follow through. Honor your promises. Say sorry when you screw up. Be kind. Be openly honest! And keep in mind that your open honesty might not always earn you the most friends, but it will always earn you the right ones.

Don't Let Anger Control You

The one who angers you controls you. We sometimes think that hatred is a weapon that attacks people we don't like, but hatred is a curved blade, and the harm we do, we also do to ourselves. Don't allow others to bring that out of you. You are bigger and better than that. You have the power to choose not to be angered and to embrace peace.

When we hang around negative people, we're pulled down. Don't waste words on people who deserve your silence. Sometimes the most powerful thing you can say is nothing at all. Learning to simply let certain people be is one of the great paths to inner peace. Forgive them, not because they deserve forgiveness, but because you deserve peace. Love yourself and free yourself of the burden of being an eternal victim, and move forward with or without them. Remember, you can't control how others act. But you can control how you respond. So let go of the grudges, resentments, and anger, and you'll feel lighter than you have in a long time.

There are countless ways to practice self-love, to take care of your mind, your body, and your emotions. All of these things are connected, and they all contribute to your overall health. If you pay attention to each of these elements of yourself, you'll soon realize your true strength is in your heart and soul. It's about having faith and trust in who you are, and a willingness to act upon it, regardless of the adversities and judgments you've faced.

This minute decide to never again beg anyone for the love, respect, and attention you should be showing yourself. Today, look at yourself in the mirror and say, "I love you, and from now on, I'm going to prove it!" When you practice self-love and self-care, you give yourself the opportunity to be happy. And when you are happy, you become a better friend, a better lover, a better family member, and a better *you*.

An Open Letter to Those Who Always Put Themselves Last

We've covered a lot of ground already in this chapter, but we want to leave you with an open letter we wrote recently that was inspired by a short email we received from one of our newest course students:

> *Dear Marc and Angel,*
>
> *I'm in my early forties and facing a troubling reality. I'm a nurse by profession and spend literally 90 percent of my time every day helping others, but somehow I've completely neglected myself in the process, and I'm feeling the pain for doing so. I feel like a siren has sounded inside my mind that I just haven't responded to. I'm often anxious and miserable, especially on my days off. What should I do? How do I motivate myself during these hard times? Any insight at all would be greatly appreciated.*
>
> *Sincerely,*
>
> *A Concerned Student*

Our open reply to all who put themselves last:

> Dear Concerned Student,
>
> Once upon a time, there was a village of people who lived in handmade wood houses. Fire was always a very real and present

danger. One small flame could burn the whole village into ashes within a few short hours. So the villagers developed a clever fire-fighting system.

At the first sight of smoke, a volunteer would turn on a loud siren. The moment the siren sounded, all villagers would drop everything and run to a preassigned location for fire fighting. Everyone would play a role, pumping water from wells, passing water buckets in a human chain, and throwing the water onto the fire until it was extinguished.

One day a traveler from a distant village heard the siren and asked someone on the street about it. The woman explained, "Whenever there's a fire, the siren is sounded and the fire is extinguished!"

The traveler was amazed and decided to bring this remarkable siren technology back to his own village, which also had dreadful problems with fires. He gathered all his villagers together and said, "You don't need to fear fire anymore, my friends. I have found a new way to extinguish it. Watch closely, and I shall demonstrate."

He lit a large bale of hay on fire that was sitting next to his own cottage. The flames quickly began to spread closer and closer to his home. Then he took out the siren he'd acquired and sounded it. The fire only grew in its intensity, so he sounded it again. The fire continued to grow rapidly.

"Just be patient, everyone! It should happen any moment now . . ."

In a panic he sounded the siren again and again, but still the fire grew and blazed with even more intensity. Within hours the entire village burned down to the ground, because, of course, he had misunderstood the purpose of the siren. It wasn't used to put out fires. It was simply a signal that directed the villagers to take positive action.

Let this story, and the traveler's tragic mistake, awaken your mind to this truth: each of us has a siren system inside ourselves. Like the fire siren in the story, it's a call to action, not a magical fix for the issues that urgently require your attention. If you heed the siren and let it motivate you to take positive action, you can save your own life and create a sense of purpose, peace, and resolve for yourself and those who depend on you.

The steps you need to take next won't be easy, but they will be worth it. Sometimes we have to learn (or relearn) to be our own best friends, because we fall too easily into the trap of being our own worst enemies. We love the idea of being loved and listened to by others, but we forget to love and listen to ourselves.

It's time to stop putting yourself last.

Make yourself a priority today.

Challenge yourself to listen to what your heart and mind are telling you.

Sincerely,

Marc and Angel

Closing Exercise

Divide a piece of paper into two columns. In one column, write down all the things you like about yourself—your personal strengths, difficult situations you've overcome, people whose lives you've touched, personal accomplishments, and values that increase your self-respect. On the other side, make a list of your personal weaknesses or issues that you still struggle with—perhaps you're selfish sometimes, or avoid taking responsibility, or maybe you haven't followed through with your commitments. Whatever these issues are, bring them into the light of day to be examined, and they will automatically feel less shameful.

At the end of the exercise, read both the strengths and the weaknesses columns aloud. Next, put your hand on your heart and tell yourself, "I am strong. I am weak. I am flawed. I am broken. I am learning. I am vulnerable. I am human. And despite all of this, I give myself permission to love myself unconditionally. I am a growing, evolving being who uses past mistakes as fuel for my journey of growth. I accept myself as I am, and I set an intention to become the best version of *me*."

Reread this chapter and do this exercise often. Spend time meditating on the rituals and patterns in your life that serve you and those that hold you back. Connect with the pain that disconnection from yourself has caused, and hold it gently in your awareness. By doing this, you'll grow in self-awareness, mindfulness, and self-love. And once you learn it is enough to be you, you will also learn to accept and love other people with more compassion and less judgment.

CHAPTER 5

Perspective: Find Beauty in Life's Challenges

Remember that time you thought you couldn't make it through? You did, and you'll do it again. Don't let your challenges get the best of you.

One of our readers, Colleen, emailed us several months ago to share a moment in which her perspective changed for the brighter: *"This morning, nearly five years after my husband's passing, a beautiful couple and their three kids knocked on my front door. The man smiled and said, 'Your husband was my heart donor. He saved my life. Not a single day has gone by that I don't pray for him and think of you. Thank you!'"*

Colleen went on to admit that she had been unable to see any positive side to her husband's death—until she found herself staring at one on her doorstep: *"It doesn't necessarily make things easier, but it certainly changed the way I think. I feel like a small piece of my broken heart has healed."*

And the truth is, it sometimes happens just like that. Although Colleen's experience is unique, and more than a little extraordinary, life sometimes has a way of slapping us with a good reminder that makes us shift our perspective for the better. Here's the thing, though: we don't have to wait for life to come along and change our perspective for us—we have the ability to do that ourselves, whether we realize it or not.

But in order to truly understand this power we all have, we first need to call out the myth that everything we experience firsthand is reality.

At a young age, we are often taught to question the stories and rumors we hear from other people but to fully accept what we experience firsthand. In other words, if we see it with our own eyes, hear it with our own ears, or feel it with our own two hands, then it is most certainly the whole truth. And while that may seem like a logical assumption, it's not always an accurate one.

Our inner dialogue and our mind-set have a drastic effect on how we interpret real-world life experiences. The stories we subconsciously tell ourselves don't just change how we feel inside—they actually change what we see, what we hear, what we experience, and what we believe to be true in the world around us. As a result, people can have the same experience but interpret it differently.

Perspective is everything.

Each of us may enter a shared experience with a different story echoing through our mind, and that story alters how we feel and how we interpret things every step of the way. Perspective is everything. And in a way, the stories we tell ourselves tend to narrow our perspective. When we enter an experience with a story about how life is, that tends to be all we see. Some of us have been deeply heartbroken. Some of us have lost parents, siblings, or children to accidents and illness. Some of us have dealt with infidelity. Some of us have been fired from jobs we relied on. Some of us have been discriminated against because of our gender or race. When we enter a new experience that arouses prominent memories of our own painful story from the past, it shifts our perspective in the present—it narrows it.

When a negative past experience narrows our present perspective, though, it's mostly a defense mechanism. Every day of our lives, we are presented with some level of uncertainty, and our minds try to compensate for this by clinging to stories we're already comfortable with. We use old stories and past experiences to interpret the present. And while this approach sometimes works, at other times those old stories and past experiences are completely irrelevant to the present moment, and they end up hurting us far more than they help.

In this chapter, we're going to explore some truths and tools you have at your disposal to shift your perspective for the brighter and find the beauty in life's difficulties, no matter how dark you feel about your situation.

Finding the Beauty in Life's Changes

There's a tradition in Buddhism in which monks meditate on their own death. They consider how their death would look to their family and community. But they don't think of this meditation as morbid. They practice it to change their perspective and realize how much good they have in their life—how much they have to be thankful for. Although life isn't perfect and involves struggle, the meditation allows them to see the incredible possibilities that still exist. By focusing on something we might think of as completely negative, the monks can shift their perspective and better see the positive things life has to offer.

In a similar way, when you can look back on your past and realize how much adversity you have overcome, you can leverage that to bring greater awareness to your personal strength. The pain of life's changes lies in realizing that we are not in control, that reality evolves outside of us and often doesn't meet our expectations.

First and foremost, a healthy and happy perspective means that you choose to embrace life's changes. If changes are a basic fact of life, then why resist? Why not embrace, let go, and live fully? That way, you're more able to see the beauty in life's changes. We know it's hard, but only because we're all so used to resisting. If you were to put aside your habitual resistance and judgmental impulses, could you imagine your true potential?

Making the Shift from Subconscious to Conscious

Our perspective stems from our past experiences: the adversities we've suffered, the negative and positive experiences we've gone through over the years, our previous relationships, all of these things sit in the back of our minds. When we address any given situation, we subconsciously reference all of that information. If we're not aware of our subconscious mind and how it affects us, we can make faulty snap judgments based on those prior experiences. As a result, most of the difficulty in shifting our perspective comes from not realizing that we're referencing our subconscious in the first place.

How do you reframe your perspective, then? Let's look at several examples of life situations that are challenging and painful and show how you can change your outlook on them.

Someone you respect snaps and yells at you. This person is hurting, frustrated, or angry, and is taking it out on you because you're close to them. They're reaching out, wanting to be saved from the uncontrollable, and of course they're not succeeding. Can you empathize with this? Have you ever been in their shoes? There is beauty in our parallels, our joint struggles, our interconnection as human beings. Empathize with this beautiful, hurting human being, feel their pain as they deal with the change in their life, give them your compassion, and then carry on without taking their struggles personally.

Your three-year-old (or thirteen-year-old) refuses to listen to you. Remarkably, your child is maturing and asserting her independence. She's thinking her own thoughts, and proving that she is her own human being, not just a little minion who follows orders. Have you ever been in her shoes—perhaps at work or earlier in life with your own parents? Have you ever been irritated by someone else trying to control you? There is beauty in this kind of growth and independence, this fighting spirit, this coming of age. See that beauty and smile. Appreciate it. Give your child some space to learn and grow.

You get laid off or fired by your employer. As difficult as losing your job is, it's an ending that leads to the beginning of everything that comes next. So let the heaviness of being successful be replaced by the lightness of being a beginner again. This new beginning is the start of a different story, an opportunity to refresh your life, to reinvent who you are. See the beauty in this opportunity—the freedom and liberation from a fixed routine—a solid foundation on which you can rebuild your life the way you always wanted it to be.

A close friend or family member dies. This one is tough, because we all grieve differently, and it takes time. When someone you love suddenly dies, you don't lose them all at once. You lose them gradually over weeks, months, and years—the way a person's scent slowly fades from an old jacket they used to wear. Yes, death is perhaps the most painful life change. We've dealt with the loss of siblings and best friends, so we know from experience that when you lose someone you can't imagine living without, your heart breaks wide open. You never completely get over the loss, because you will never forget them. However, in an unusual way, this is also the good news. We discussed this already in chapter 3, but it's worth restating here: death is a beginning, because while we have lost someone special, this ending, like when we lose something we cherish that's important to us, is a moment of reinvention. Although deeply sad, their passing forces us to reinvent our lives, and in this reinvention is an opportunity to experience beauty in new, unseen ways. And finally, of course, death is an opportunity to celebrate a person's life, and to be grateful for the beauty they showed us.

As you now know, we've known our share of adversity. We've struggled emotionally and financially. During those times, our expectations of how "good" our lives were supposed to be were shattered, leaving us feeling angry, bitter, and frightened. But here's the thing: our perspective on the adversity was holding us back. We kept telling ourselves we deserved exactly the life we'd imagined, but this was preventing us from moving forward. It wasn't until we started to open our minds to the beauty in the seemingly terrible that we saw new paths start to open before us.

In the next section, we'll dig a little deeper into some of the biggest truths that we need to recognize in order to become masters of our own perspective, no matter the situation.

The Five Life-Changing Truths Most People Are Too Scared (or Too Stubborn) to Admit

Although it may be tough to stretch our comfort zones beyond the boundaries of what we're familiar with—and into the realities of what we don't yet feel ready to face—doing so is often the clearest path to mental and emotional freedom. Becoming mentally and emotionally free makes it easier to step back from a difficult situation and view it from a more constructive perspective.

But too many of us, for much of our lives, embrace half-truths and falsehoods that get in the way, preventing us from growing, learning, and living our greatest potential. Facing down these falsehoods can be downright uncomfortable, scary, and even painful— but it's also absolutely necessary. With that in mind, we want to highlight five incredibly beneficial, life-changing truths that have helped hundreds of our course students and coaching clients see through the falsehoods that were blocking them from embracing a new, healthier perspective.

1. **The vast majority of our struggles are self-created, and we can choose to overcome them in an instant.**

    We all struggle. We all suffer on the inside. Every day, we worry. We procrastinate. We feel overwhelmed, angry, lonely, and not good enough. We wish we were thinner, had more money, had different jobs or different relationships. We think everything in life should be easier.

And yet, every one of these struggles is self-created. They are real, but they are only real because we have created them in our minds. We have attached ourselves to certain ideals and fantasies about how life has to be in order for it to be good enough for us. We worry because things might not turn out how we expect. We procrastinate because we fear discomfort and failure. We feel overwhelmed because we think we should be further along than we are. We feel angry because we think life should be different.

But it doesn't have to be this way. Because our struggles are all in our heads. Instead, take a deep breath, let all that thinking and ruminating go, and bring your attention to the present moment. Focus on what's here with you now—the light, the sounds, your body, the ground under your feet, the objects and people moving and resting around you. Don't judge these things against what they should be—just accept what they actually are. See life as it is, without all the ideals and fantasies. Let go of all of those stressful distractions, and experience the moment you're in, realizing that it's good enough as it is.

2. **We fear the judgments of others, even though those judgments are rarely valid or significant.**

"What's wrong with wanting other people to like you?" That's a question our students and clients ask us frequently. In a nutshell, tying your self-worth to everyone else's opinions gives you a flawed sense of reality that can cause serious trouble when it comes to your confidence and happiness. Yet we do it all the time. From wanting others to think we're attractive, to checking the number of likes and comments on our social media posts, most of us care a whole lot about what others think.

As we grow up, we learn to separate our thoughts and emotions from everyone else's, but many of us continue to seek—even beg for—positive social validation from others. In a recent survey we did with twelve hundred of our students and clients, two-thirds admitted that their self-worth was strongly tied to what other people thought of them. And even though that isn't a healthy way to measure your self-worth, it isn't surprising that so many of us think this way. We naturally respond to everything we experience through the lens of our learned expectations—a set of deep-rooted beliefs about the way the world is and how things should be.

One of the most prevailing expectations we have involves external validation and how others "should" respond to us. More than a century ago, sociologist Charles Cooley identified the phenomenon of the "looking-glass self," which is when we believe "I am not what I think I am, and I am not what you think I am—I am what I think that you think I am." Sadly, this kind of external validation has insecurity at its core, and relying on it for even a short time chips away at our self-confidence and self-worth.

The biggest problem is that we tend to forget that people judge us based on a collection of influences in their own life that have nothing to do with us. Basing your self-worth on what others think puts you in a perpetual state of vulnerability—you are literally at the mercy of their unreliable, biased perspectives.

3. **Our past experiences have conditioned us to believe we are less capable than we are.**

A metaphor comes in handy for this one: zookeepers typically strap a thin metal chain to a grown elephant's leg and then attach the other end to a small wooden peg that's hammered into the ground. The ten-foot-tall, ten-thousand-pound elephant could easily snap the chain, uproot the wooden peg, and escape to freedom with minimal effort. But it doesn't. In fact, the elephant never even tries. The world's most powerful land animal, which can uproot a big tree as easily as you could break a toothpick, remains defeated by a small wooden peg and a flimsy chain.

Why? Because when the elephant was a baby, its trainers used the same methods to domesticate it. At the time, the chain and peg were strong enough to restrain the baby elephant. When it tried to break away, the metal chain would pull it back. Soon the baby elephant realized that trying to escape was impossible. So it stopped trying. And now that the elephant is fully grown, it sees the chain and the peg and it remembers what it learned as a baby—that the chain and peg are impossible to escape. Of course this is no longer true, but it doesn't matter. It doesn't matter that the two-hundred-pound baby is now a ten-thousand-pound powerhouse. The elephant's self-limiting thoughts and beliefs prevail.

If you think about it, we are all like elephants. We all have incredible power inside us. And we have our own chains and pegs—the self-limiting thoughts and beliefs that hold us back. Sometimes it's a childhood experience or an old failure. Sometimes it's something we were told when we were younger. The key thing to realize is this: we need to learn from the past, but also to be willing to change our assumptions—our perspective—about the way things are now. Life is not static. You *can* break free.

4. **Real pain, heartbreak, and failure are experiences that can help us grow.**

Many of the most iconic novels, songs, and inventions of all time were inspired by gut-wrenching pain, heartbreak, or failure. The silver lining of these great challenges is that they were catalysts for the creation of epic masterpieces.

An emerging field of psychological research called *post-traumatic growth* has suggested that most people are able to use their hardships and traumas for substantial creative and intellectual development. Specifically, researchers have found that trauma can help people develop their long-term contentment, emotional strength, and resourcefulness.

When our view of the world has been shattered, we are forced to change our perspective. We suddenly have the opportunity to look out and see things with fresh eyes. This is a healthy way to cope with a changing worldview. So rather than shy away from unexpected changes, fully embrace reality and the broad range of experiences you encounter on the road of life, taking the good with the bad. This includes all of your emotions, ups and downs, blissful moments and painful ones, and everything in between. Life is intricate, complicated, and remarkable.

Fully embracing life in this way means opening yourself to unimaginable possibilities, becoming vulnerable to unexpected changes, being compassionate with yourself when times are tough, giving yourself some extra love and kindness no matter what happens, and being grateful for the opportunity to experience it all. It means not expecting always to be the perfect human living the perfect life, but instead accepting reality as it is, and accepting yourself as you are, then making the best of it.

5. **We have to give up some things to get what we ultimately want in life.**

This might be one of the hardest truths to swallow, and that's why we mention it several times throughout this book. We have to say no to good things to be able to say yes to important things. We simply can't do it all. So be mindful, and choose wisely. What you choose to focus on grows stronger in your life. At every moment, thousands of little things are competing for your attention. All of these things fall into one of two categories: things that are priorities and things that are not.

Focus on the few key things that are most important for you to succeed today—to take another small step forward. And remember that giving up other things isn't just about making small, immediate sacrifices; it's also about gradually gaining the resources you need to do something significant. If you want to achieve an important goal or outcome in your life, you have to give up the things that conflict with it. This doesn't mean you have to intentionally suffer. It just means you can't have it all—you have to sacrifice something that you value less than whatever it is you ultimately want to achieve.

When you fail to realize the five truths above, you can end up with a skewed perspective of your worth, your capabilities, and your ability to overcome adversity. But if you can remember these points, especially when you find yourself face-to-face with a difficult situation, you'll be much better equipped to keep your perspective on track whenever life throws you a curveball.

Mastering the Art of Self-Inquiry

Albert Einstein once said, "The world as we have created it is a process of our thinking. It cannot be changed without changing our thinking."

The mind is your battleground. It's the place where your fiercest and most ruthless conflict resides. It's where hundreds of negative outcomes you thought were going to happen were just fantasies. It's where your expectations always get the best of you. The mind is where you fall victim to your own train of thought time and again. But if you allow these thoughts to linger in your mind, they will succeed in stripping you of happiness, stability, and ultimately your life. You will think yourself into tears, bouts of depression, and utter defeat. Let this be your wake-up call!

You are what you think. You can't change anything if you can't change your

You are what you think.

thinking. A beautiful day begins with a beautiful mindset. When you wake up, take a second to think about what a privilege it is simply to be alive and healthy. Breathe onto the bathroom mirror, just to see how amazing your breath looks. The moment you start acting like life is a blessing, we assure you it will start to feel like one.

One of the strategies we teach over and over again is self-inquiry—the art of asking ourselves the right questions. Why is this strategy so important? Because the questions we ask ourselves become thoughts. Thoughts then become words. Words become actions. Actions become character. And character changes everything. When times get tough and big problems arise, as they inevitably will, it is the strength of our character that sees us through.

And since our character is directly influenced by what we ask and say to ourselves on a daily basis, we want you to think about how you've been speaking to yourself lately. Have you been using the empowering, encouraging words you would speak to someone you respect? Or the belittling remarks you would shout to an enemy if you had no filter? All day long, you speak silently to yourself—and a part of you believes every word. That's why it's important to stay mindful when problems arise, and meditate on these questions:

What do I need to stop thinking and saying to myself? Stop discrediting yourself for everything you aren't, and start giving yourself credit for everything you *are*. We have to learn to be our own best friends, because sometimes we fall too easily into the trap of being our own worst enemies.

Will I blame others and deny responsibility? Or will you create an action plan to move forward on your own terms? Imagine how much more happy and effective you'd be if instead of denying, blaming, dreading, and fighting certain situations and tasks, you simply handled them.

How can I respond from a place of clarity and strength rather than reactivity? Every time you are tempted to react in the same old way, ask yourself if you want to be a prisoner of the past or a pioneer of the future. And remember that our character is often most evident in our highs and lows. Be humble at the mountaintops, be strong in the valleys, and be faithful in between.

Am I placing unnecessary expectations on myself or others? Expectations are like fine pottery—the harder you hold on to them, the more likely they are to crack. Remember this. You will find life a lot easier when you adjust your expectations. Let go a little, and appreciate your life and relationships for what they are.

Who, or what, needs my forgiveness? Forgiveness doesn't always lead to healed relationships and situations; some relationships and situations aren't meant to be. But forgive anyway, and let what's meant to be, *be*. Go ahead and set yourself free. When you hold resentment, you are bound to that person or condition by an emotional link that is stronger than steel. Forgiveness is the only way to dissolve that link and break free.

What do I know better for next time? Don't let your fear of past events affect the outcome of your future. Live for what today has to offer, not what yesterday has taken away. There will always be obstacles, but we are confined most often by the walls we build ourselves. What we see depends on how we look at it. Forget what you've lost and focus on what you've learned.

Life is full of uncontrollable circumstances; the only thing we can control is how we choose to respond. When you take the time to think about it, everything happening around us is neutral and meaningless until we give it meaning. And the questions we ask ourselves drive the meaning we create.

Sometimes things have to go very wrong before they can go right. Our most significant opportunities are often found in times of great difficulty. In a terrible economic recession, Angel lost the breadwinning job she'd had for eight years. Initially, she was devastated, because she couldn't find another job at all. She felt that she had been wronged, and all the rejections made her feel like she didn't have experience that would be beneficial to anyone. She felt completely defeated.

But then she started asking herself the right questions, and slowly began to realize that she—that both of us—had a chance to begin again. She began to shift her perspective from feeling wronged and victimized, and started to see the potential opportunities in losing her job. She and I soon understood that we now had no reason to stay in our hometown, so we packed up a few of our belongings and moved across the country to a better job market. The move accelerated the success of our blog and business and helped us cope with our other adversities, and Angel started working at a university where she was able to get her master's degree for free.

Surely there's a lot of details we're skipping over here, but the point is that almost every experience helps you grow over time, even if it's hard to see in the moment. Circumstances will direct you, correct you, and perfect you over time. Sometimes these circumstances knock you down. You might feel as though you'll be trapped in a rut forever, but remember this: *you won't*. For Angel, knowing that she always has control over her perspective is an ongoing challenge, as it is for all of us. But radically shifting her perspective about what happened to her ultimately helped her turn a challenge into a success.

What to Remember When Everything Goes Wrong

In our office, there's a framed entry from Marc's grandmother's journal, dated September 16, 1977. It reads:

> Today I'm sitting in my hospital bed waiting to have both my breasts removed. But in a strange way, I feel like the lucky one. Until now I have had no health problems. I'm a sixty-nine-year-old woman in the last room at the end of the hall before the pediatric division of the hospital begins. Over the past few hours I have watched dozens of cancer patients being wheeled by in wheelchairs and rolling beds. None of these patients could be a day older than seventeen.

This journal entry is displayed in our office because it continues to remind us that there is always, *always* something to be thankful for. And that no matter how good or bad we have it, we must wake up each day thankful for our lives, because someone, somewhere is desperately fighting for theirs.

We recently celebrated the thirty-fifth birthday of Angel's childhood best friend, Janet. Four years ago, she was diagnosed with stage 2 breast cancer—devastating news for anyone, and especially for someone so young. Thankfully, she's now in remission and has been cancer free for the past two years. When we were at lunch, she told us, "I am loving my thirties so much more than my twenties. I'm more confident, I know what I want out of life, know what my capabilities are. I know that life is limited, and that I only get this one life, and I'm doing my best to make the best of each and every day."

Hearing her say those words was remarkable, because we saw how her perspective on the situation allowed her to view a horribly difficult time as an opportunity to understand what she wanted out of life. Her example reminded us that happiness is not the absence of problems, but the ability to use them as opportunities to change your perspective for the better. Think about your own life. What joy and opportunities might you see more clearly if your mind weren't holding on so tightly to your struggles and disappointments? Remember, it's not what the world takes away from you that counts; it's what you do with what you have left.

Here are a few simple reminders to help shift your perspective when you need it most:

Pain is part of growing. Sometimes life closes doors because it's time to move forward. And that's a good thing, because we often won't move unless circumstances force us to. When times are tough, remind yourself that no pain comes without a purpose. Move on from what hurt you, but never forget what it taught you. Just because you're struggling doesn't mean you're failing. Every great success requires some type of worthy struggle to get there. Good things take time, so stay patient and stay positive.

Everything in life is temporary. Every time it rains, the sun always comes out again. Every time you get hurt, you heal. After darkness, there is always light—we are reminded of this every morning, but still we often forget, and instead choose to believe that the night will last forever. Every moment gives you a new beginning and a new ending. You get another chance every second. You have to take it and make the best of it.

Worrying and complaining change nothing. Those who complain the most accomplish the least. It's always better to attempt to do something great and fail than to do nothing. It's not over if you've lost; it's over when you do nothing but complain about it. If you believe in something, keep trying. Don't let the shadows of the past darken the doorstep of your future. Spending today complaining about yesterday won't make tomorrow any brighter. Start being grateful for all the problems you don't have.

Your scars are symbols of your strength. Rumi wrote, "The wound is the place where the light enters you." Nothing could be closer to the truth. Out of suffering have emerged the strongest souls; the most powerful characters in this great world are seared with scars. Don't ever be ashamed of the scars life has left you with. A scar means the hurt is over and the wound is closed. It means you conquered the pain, learned a lesson, grew stronger, and moved forward. You can't make the scars in your life disappear, but you *can* change the way you see them.

Every little struggle is a step forward. In life, patience is not about waiting; it's the ability to keep a good attitude while working hard on your dreams, knowing that the work is worth it. So if you're going to try, put in the time and go all the way. This could mean losing stability and comfort for a while, and maybe even your mind on occasion. It could mean stretching your comfort zone so thin it gives you a nonstop case of the chills. It could mean sacrificing relationships and all that's familiar. It could mean criticism from your peers. It could mean walking alone for a while. But if you want it, you'll do it, despite the possibilities of failure, rejection, and discomfort. And every step will feel better than anything else you can imagine. You will realize that the struggle is not found on the path; it *is* the path. And it's worth it.

Other people's negativity is not your problem. Be positive even when negativity surrounds you. When other people treat you poorly, keep being you. Don't ever let someone else's bitterness change the person you are. Instead, think of them as a reminder of how *not* to be, and maintain your enthusiasm and focus. Above all, don't ever change just to impress someone who says you're not good enough. People are going to talk regardless of what you do or how well you do it. If you believe strongly in something, don't be afraid to fight for it. Great strength comes from overcoming what others think is impossible.

What's meant to be will be. True strength comes when you have so much to cry and complain about, but you prefer to smile and appreciate your life instead. There are blessings hidden in every struggle you face, but you have to be willing to open your heart and mind to see them. You can't force things to happen. You can only drive yourself crazy trying. In the end, loving your life is about trusting your intuition, taking chances, losing and finding happiness, cherishing the memories, and learning through experience. It's a long-term journey. You have to stop worrying, wondering, and doubting every step of the way. You might not end up exactly where you intended to go, but you will eventually arrive precisely where you need to be.

The best thing you can do is keep going. Don't be afraid to get back up—to try again, to love again, to live again, and to dream again. Don't let a difficult lesson harden your heart. Life's best lessons are often learned at the toughest times and from the biggest mistakes. There will be occasions when it seems like everything that could possibly go wrong is going wrong. And you might feel like you will be stuck in this rut forever, but you won't. When you feel like quitting, remember that sometimes things have to go very wrong before they can go right. Sometimes you have to endure the worst to arrive at your best.

You Are Not Alone

In the midst of bad days and hard times, it's easy to look around and see a bunch of people who seem to have figured everything out. But we assure you they haven't. We're all struggling in our own unique way every single day. And if we could just be brave enough to open up about it and talk to each other more often, we'd realize that we are not alone in feeling lost and alone with our issues.

So many of us are fighting a similar battle right now. Try to remember this. No matter how embarrassed or pathetic you feel about your own situation, there are others out there experiencing the same emotions. When you hear yourself say, "I am all alone," it's just your troubled subconscious mind trying to sell you a lie.

There's always someone who can relate to you.

There's always someone who understands.

Perhaps you can't immediately talk to them, but they are out there. We are out there right now.

Here are a few reminders we often examine with our clients who are struggling to feel less alone with what's weighing them down.

1. **Every passing face on the street represents a story just as captivating, complicated, and crazy as yours.**

    When you look at another person, any person, remember that everyone has a story. Everyone has gone through something that's inadvertently changed them and forced them to grow. Everyone you meet has struggled, and continues to struggle in some way, and to them it's just as hard as what you're going through.

    Marc was lucky enough to have a very wise grandmother who coached him through this reality when he was just a teenager. Here's what she told him when he was struggling to understand his anxieties and desperately hoping to fit in:

    "If you think you know someone who never feels the way you do right now—who never feels a bit lost and alone, and downright confused and crazy—you just don't know enough about them. Every one of us contains a measure of 'crazy' that moves us in strange, often perplexing ways. This side of us is necessary; it's part of our human ability to think, adapt, and grow. It's part of being intelligent," she said. "No great mind has ever existed without a touch of this kind of madness."

    She continued, "And sometimes how you feel simply won't align with how you want to feel—it's mostly just your subconscious mind's way of helping you look at things from a different perspective. These feelings will come and go quickly as

*long as you let them go . . . as long as you consciously
acknowledge them, and then push through them. At least that's
what I've learned to do for myself, out of necessity, on a very
regular basis. So you and I are actually struggling through this
one together, honey. And I'm also pretty certain we're not the
only ones."*

2. **You are far more than that broken piece of you.**

When times are tough, and some piece of you is
chipped and broken, it's easy to feel like everything—*all* of
you—is broken along with it. But that's not true.

We all have this picture in our minds of ourselves—this
idea of what kind of person we are. When this idea gets
even slightly harmed or threatened, we react defensively
and often irrationally. People may question whether we
did a good job, and this threatens our idea of being a
competent person, so we become angry or hurt by the
criticism. Someone falsely accuses us of something and this
damages our idea that we're a good person, so we get
angry and attack the other person, or we cower and cry.
And the list goes on.

But the craziest thing is, often we are actually the ones
harming and threatening ourselves with negativity and
false accusations.

Recently Marc was struggling to motivate himself to
work on a new creative project he'd been procrastinating
about, so his view of himself as someone who's always
productive and motivated and has great ideas suddenly
came under attack. When he realized he wasn't getting
things done, it made him feel terribly self-conscious and
uncertain because he began worrying that he wasn't who

he thought he was—a scary feeling. And this in turn made him feel very alone inside.

His solution was to realize that he's not just one thing. He's not always productive—sometimes he is, but sometimes he's unproductive too. He's not always motivated—sometimes he is, but other times he's not. And obviously he doesn't always have great ideas either—because that would be impossible.

The truth is, he came to realize, *I can be many things, and remembering this helps me stretch my identity so it's not so fragile—so it doesn't completely shatter when a small piece of it gets chipped. Then it doesn't matter if someone occasionally thinks I didn't do a good job, or if I sometimes catch myself not doing a good job—because I don't always do a good job.*

I make mistakes.

I am less than perfect.

And that's perfectly okay.

We'd like to end this chapter by directly addressing our fellow souls out there who are tired and struggling to find happiness at this very moment, seemingly alone.

This one's for you.

We want you to know that we understand. Life is not always easy. Every day can be an unpredictable challenge. Some days it can be difficult just to get out of bed in the morning, to face reality and put on that smile. But we want you to know that your smile—just knowing you're out there somewhere—has kept us going on more days than we can count. Never forget that, even when times get tough, as they sometimes will, you are incredible, you really are.

You won't always be perfect and neither will we. Because

nobody is perfect, and nobody deserves to be perfect. Everybody has issues. No one has it easy. We are all fighting our own unique battles. But we are fighting them simultaneously together.

And remember, courage doesn't always growl like a lion. Sometimes it's just a quiet purr at the end of the day whispering, "I will try my best again tomorrow." So stand strong. Things always turn out best for people who make the best out of the way things turn out.

And we are committed to making the best of it along with you.

One day at a time, one tiny step at a time, for the rest of our lives.

Yes, life is tough, but so are you. Find the strength to smile every day. Find the courage to feel different but beautiful. Find it in your heart to continue making others smile too. Don't stress over things you can't change. Live simply. Love generously. Speak truthfully. Work diligently. And even if you fall short, keep going . . . and growing.

Closing Exercise

As we've discussed throughout this chapter, perspective is about finding the silver lining in any given situation and using it to take your next positive step forward. It's all about finding the beauty in things. If you're gearing yourself up for failure, you're hardwiring your brain to expect just that. Instead, practice looking for the positive. This can be a difficult thing to do, one that takes time and practice. The key is to focus a little less on managing your *problems* and a little more on managing your *mindset*. Here are three simple questions you can

> Practice looking for the positive.

use to help you do that and shift your perspective in the right direction:

- What could I be grateful for right now, if I really wanted to be grateful?
- What could I smile about right now, if I really wanted to smile?
- What could I be excited about right now, if I really wanted to get excited?

Again, asking yourself the right questions can make any difficult situation more manageable and less frightening. It's an ongoing practice, but it teaches us that our perspective—whether we choose to make it work for us or against us—is entirely within our control.

CHAPTER 6

Getting Unstuck: Embrace Change and Take Action When Necessary

Change is the only constant, so learn to embrace it.

For years, Angel wrestled with the fact that she was adopted. She hadn't seen her biological mother since she was a baby, and with every passing year, the subconscious fear that she might never meet her grew stronger. One thought constantly lingered at the back of Angel's mind: what if her biological mother died before she had the chance to talk to her?

In some ways, Angel was ashamed of being adopted, so she hid that part of herself because she felt that she didn't have anyone to talk to or identify with about it. And it didn't help that the majority of the stories she heard about her biological mother were negative. As a result, the opinions of others dictated Angel's thoughts and feelings, making it difficult for Angel to form her own opinion about reaching out to her. The situation weighed heavily on Angel's heart and mind, and not taking action to get in touch began to eat away at her.

Although she'd had her biological mother's phone number for more than two years, she was endlessly reluctant to make the call. Finally, she asked herself: what's *really* holding me back?

Extremely nervous, Angel called, expecting the worst. But what happened was far from it: they talked for an hour, and Angel walked away from the conversation feeling lighter and more at peace—finally able to let go of the burden of not making the call. By taking control of her situation, Angel realized the power she had over the story she was telling herself. Rather than waiting for her mother to reach out to her, she took action. She erased the fear and worry of many years in just one hour, simply by following through on her decision.

Many of our clients come to us with a problem similar to Angel's: they feel stuck in their current situation. Some of them even recognize that nothing exceptionally tragic has happened to them, but they still feel unhappy or unfulfilled with their life the way it is and don't know how to take action to change things. They have opportunities available, but they aren't actively pursuing them. They're procrastinating, telling themselves that achieving these new possibilities would be too painful or too much work. In other words, they persistently avoid the changes they need to make.

Although shying away from the potential agony of change can provide the illusion of comfort, this kind of passive interaction with life ultimately leads to unhappiness. We aren't strangers to feeling this way. We know exactly what it's like to look at an opportunity and shy away from it, simply because we're scared to see what the outcome might be. We know that change and growth can be uncomfortable. We also know that in the end, nothing is as painful as staying stuck somewhere you don't belong. It takes a great deal of courage to admit that something needs to change, and a lot more courage still to accept the responsibility for making the change happen. But doing so is worth every bit of effort you can muster.

In the previous chapter, we talked about how much control you have over your perspective. Perspective is crucial, but so is action. Sometimes, in order to get back to happy, you need to make real changes in your life—to "unstick" yourself from a current situation that's not serving you. This chapter is all about why it's so important to embrace change, and how you can take small steps to do just that.

First, we're going to discuss the warning signs of being stuck that ultimately mean it's time to make a change in your life.

The Signs It's Time to Change Your Situation

In chapter 5, we put the lie to the myth that everything you experience firsthand is true. We want to explode another myth here: that you have to wait for the "right time" to make a change in your life. The truth is, it's never too late or too early to be who you are capable of being. There's no time limit on when you can start living the life you've always dreamed of. There is no mythical door that shuts after you turn a certain age, blocking you off from experiencing the things you want to do.

Human beings are experts at trying to avoid change, but change avoidance is one of the biggest factors that leads to unhappiness. When we find ourselves in situations that challenge our self-perception, we often react by feeling trapped or on guard. We often think that the worst thing that could happen is that the status quo will be interrupted. But who wants to spend their life thinking and feeling this way?

Happily, life has a way of throwing up red flags when it's time for us to make a change—we just have to be watchful for them. With that in mind, take a look at this list and ask yourself: are any of these the reasons I'm unhappy with my life as it is now?

1. **Fear is holding you back.** When you're scared of something, realize that fear is the worst of it; fear itself is your real enemy. So get up, get out in the stormy weather of the real world, and face your fear. Do so by staring at it dead in the eyes and then walking right through it into the storm. Let the rain kiss your skin. That's the first step. Because no one who's wet fears the rain. And from that point, you can make a much smarter decision about what to do next.

2. **You catch yourself feeding the negative.** There is always a fierce battle between two hungry forces going on inside each of us. One is negative—fear, anger, jealousy, greed, resentment, dishonesty, and hatred. The other is positive—love, joy, peace, hope, compassion, kindness, and truth. The force that wins is the one you feed the most.

3. **Your mind is everywhere except right here, right now.** Some people believe the past is endless, the future is endless, and the present is a moment. But the truth is, *the past is a moment, the future is a moment, and the present is endless.* Make sure you're living in it and making the most of this present moment we call life.

4. **You feel pressured to be someone other than yourself.** Some people simply will not like it when you are being yourself. They will always be more comfortable with the

person they imagined you to be. So when they disapprove of you, ignore them. Because what makes you happy supersedes what they think will make you happy. Do not disown your truth. Do not fear your originality. Do not live in their opinions. Decide that you matter, and that there is nothing wrong with just being *you*.

5. **You feel like you're competing against everyone else.** You are in competition with no one but yourself. You are running your own race. You have no need to play the game of being better than anyone in any way, shape, or form. Just aim to improve—to be better than you were yesterday. This is the mindset that will set you free.

6. **A relationship is making you miserable.** You can't change all the people around you, but you can change which people you choose to be around. No relationship is worth being miserable over every day of your life. Sometimes you have to distance yourself for a while. And sometimes you just have to erase the messages, delete the numbers, and move on. You don't have to forget who they once were, but you do have to accept that they aren't the same person anymore—and neither are you.

7. **You feel bored.** Don't say you're bored with your situation; it's a useless thing to say. You live in a vast world that you've seen only a small fraction of. And even the inside of your own mind is endless—it literally goes on forever to depths you've never explored. The fact that you are alive is amazing, so you don't really have a reason to be bored. If you are, you know it's time to make a change.

8. **You've been resisting change.** Change isn't part of the process; it is the process. The bad news: nothing is permanent. The good news: nothing is permanent. Truly, *nothing* is permanent! When you understand that, you can do almost anything you wish, because you're not trying to hold on to anything anymore.

9. **Other people are writing your story for you.** Your life is a story, and you are the protagonist. Everyone else, and we mean *everyone*, is a side character. No other character has the power to stress you out unless you let them. This is just a friendly reminder to help you get unstuck and move your story along. Live your story the way you want to live it, and don't let anyone else write the ending for you.

If any of these resonate with you, you certainly aren't alone. Many people are afraid to step forward and change their situation simply because they don't know how or because they're afraid to fail. Remember, it's always better to take an imperfect step forward than to take no step at all.

How to Change Your Situation for the Better

As we said, waiting for the "right time" to change your situation is only going to hold you back. The myth of perfect timing prevents so many of us from moving forward and achieving our true potential simply because we believe we aren't good enough, or ready enough, at any given moment. Not only is this belief detrimental to your growth as a human being, it's a built-in excuse not to try.

Rarely is life going to work out perfectly, and rarely will the stars align. If you're waiting around to gather all the resources you *think* you need to take the next step forward, before you know it, you will have wasted all the time you have.

So what's the alternative? It's recognizing that changing your situation is about taking action in the present. It's about asking yourself: what are the things I can do to improve this situation *now*? It's coming to terms with the ideas and thoughts in your head that are holding you back. It's about deciding that you are going to stop waiting, stop making excuses, and start making changes, however small they may be. Changing your situation is about being mindful of what you want to change—and then finding the *one thing* you can do first to improve it. That one action might not change everything, but it will put you on the path to something better.

Getting Back to Happy Takes Lots of Small Steps

Although the idea of perfect timing is a myth that can prevent us from taking action, the actions we take still need to be smart ones. One way to start taking smarter actions is by making them *smaller*. We'll use an example to illustrate what we mean.

Let's pull a wild example out of a hat: let's say you're tired of the drudgery of the eight-to-five and want to start your own business. If you don't have a family that depends on you or a lot of financial responsibilities, then it may be easier for you to start taking big, immediate steps toward leaving your job and building that business. On the other hand, if you have people who rely on you financially, to suddenly quit your job and leap 100 percent into a new venture probably would be irresponsible.

But if changing your situation in this way—leaving behind the rat race to become a business owner—is important to you, then *not* doing anything would also be irresponsible, and that's the key. Don't wait endlessly for something to change on its own just because you have constraints. Instead of taking a giant leap, there still may be small steps you can take toward your goal that aren't going to upend your entire life and cause even more pain. Focus on adjusting your lifestyle incrementally, and building in a little flexibility, to better accommodate opportunities that arise. By taking small steps, you'll be taking action and better equipping yourself eventually to strike out on a whole new path.

What might this look like in our scenario of the wannabe entrepreneur? A great way to start taking those small steps would be by asking yourself: how can I begin to set up my lifestyle so I can start making these shifts? From a financial aspect, it might be saving up one or two years' worth of savings or paying down some debt. It could also be sharing your plans with your family and friends, to obtain their guidance and support for the plan you have in mind. Remember: your support system is invaluable! (But do make sure that your support system is actually supportive.)

The bottom line is this: whether it's building a business or making any other life change, the key to moving from procrastination to progress is realizing that you don't have to have everything figured out when you start. By taking small steps, you'll be able to learn as you go, gradually collecting information that will help you understand if this is truly the right path for you or if you need to change direction. This approach sets up a feedback loop that provides the input that will help you course correct as you navigate toward the life you want.

After all, there's a good chance that the person who wants to build a side business gets a year down the road and realizes that the dream they had was the wrong dream. What they want now is something different. Maybe it's slightly different, or maybe it's drastically different, but it's different. And the small steps they've taken to get to that point have helped them get to that crucial realization in a smart way. They've also come to see that even if they changed direction—or changed their mind entirely—all the passion and effort they put in along the way is still progress that's gotten them closer to being at peace with a life explored and well lived.

Of course, taking small steps and adjusting as you go can sometimes put you at odds with "the ways things are done." For example, in our society, we often tell teenagers to go to college and to pick a career path that will satisfy them for the next forty years of their life. That's a joke, because that's not necessarily what getting a degree is about. It's about educating yourself and being prepared to take small steps forward. It's about earning a degree you can use to test the waters in an ocean of possibility, then making shifts as you begin to better understand yourself and the life you want to create.

The truth is, no one wins a game of chess by only moving forward; sometimes you have to move backward to put yourself in a position to win. And this is a perfect metaphor for life. Sometimes when it feels like you're running into one dead end after another, it's actually a sign that you're not on the right path. Maybe you were meant to hang a left back when you took a right, and that's perfectly fine. Life gradually teaches us that U-turns are allowed.

Changing Your Situation Requires Sacrifice and Discomfort

Taking small steps can make a big difference, but there's no getting around the fact that changing your situation is often uncomfortable. That's why many people, including us, often don't do it—at least not initially. But we have to catch ourselves and remind ourselves that just because it isn't easy doesn't mean that it isn't worth it. The key is to remember that it's okay to feel uncomfortable, because that's where human growth begins.

In order to get something in life, we often have to give something up. In order to change our situation, we have to take some action that's not necessarily going to be easy or fun. Life is the opposite of perfection. It can be beautiful, of course, but it's also messy and chaotic. Too often we shy away from pursuing our passions because we're afraid they might not be worth the discomfort involved in making a change. It's scary and uncomfortable to upset the status quo, even when it's in service of something better.

It all comes back to a single question: *What is worth suffering for?* Is the change you're about to implement—be it ending a relationship, leaving a job, or something else—truly going to help you move toward the life you want to lead? If so, then it's probably worth enduring some pain and discomfort to get there. You can also rephrase the question to help you think through it: How important is this goal or passion to you? And what are you willing to sacrifice, in the short term and long term, in order to be happier in the long term?

By questioning your situation like this, you'll realize that there are great reasons to step out of your comfort zone and to suffer. Changes of this magnitude do not come easily for any of us, and we understand that. But once you start to have an honest conversation with yourself about what you want to change in your life, you'll find it easier to direct your full energy toward reaching those goals and overcoming your obstacles. When you're focused on all the good that will come from making the change you desire, the sacrifices you'll have to make to achieve that change simply won't seem as big a deal. Or if the sacrifices seem too big, perhaps the change isn't right for you.

In any case, adapting to change, and getting unstuck from an unhappy situation, is fundamentally about becoming comfortable with discomfort. It's about choosing to embrace that discomfort, not because we want to make our lives overly complicated or difficult, but because there are some things that are worth suffering for. It's about suffering a little bit in the moment, or in smaller areas of your life, in order to suffer a lot less in the long run. It's about giving certain things up to get more of what you truly want in life!

> There are some things that are worth suffering for.

No doubt, if you want those six-pack abs, you also have to want the hard workouts and the healthy meals. If you want the successful business, you also have to want the long days, the stressful business deals and decisions, and the possibility of failing twenty times to learn what you need to know to succeed in the long run. You simply have to give up certain ideals, comforts, routines, and so on to get what you ultimately want.

And again, remember that giving things up isn't just about making small, immediate sacrifices. It's also about gradually gaining the resources you need to do something significant. When you give something up, you automatically create an opening in your life for something else. By saying no to everything that's not aligned with your priorities, you make room for what is.

In chapter 3 we said that if you want to achieve a significant goal or outcome in your life, you have to give up the things that conflict with it. This doesn't mean you have to make your life unnecessarily grueling. It just means you can't have it all—you have to sacrifice something that you value less than whatever you ultimately want to achieve. For example, you might sacrifice some level of comfort in the present for a better chance of future achievement. Here are a few additional, real-world examples:

- Last year, one of our course students gave up a sizable salary at an office job for a commission-based sales job in an industry she's passionate about. She stalled on making this transition for the longest time because she feared not having a steady paycheck. Indeed, for the first six months her commission paycheck was lower, but now her income is nearly double what she used to make at her old office job, and she loves what she does for a living.

- Another one of our course students made losing twenty-five pounds her New Year's resolution, so she gave up a little sleep and some junk food, and embraced the mornings in the gym, the sore muscles, and the healthy meals her resolution required. And with a little support and accountability from us, she was able to hit her target weight in under six months.

- Angel and I gave up living on the beach in San Diego in a really cool, walkable neighborhood. Even though we were initially reluctant to leave, we now live in South Florida, where we get to watch the joy in Marc's parents' eyes on a daily basis as they play in the yard with our son, and their only grandson, Mac. You really can't put a price tag on that.

If you want something in life, you have to embrace the costs of getting it; you have to be willing to make certain sacrifices. And it's up to you, and *only you*, to decide if the benefits are worth the cost.

What You Might Need to Give Up in Order to Move Forward

When our best friend Josh died, as difficult as the news of his death was to swallow, we intellectually knew nothing would bring him back. But it still felt emotionally easiest to get lost in our grief and mull over the idea of never losing him—far easier than actually confronting what his loss meant to us. So that's precisely what we did for a while—we fantasized about not losing him and bringing him back—until we suffered a bout of moderate depression. Thankfully, in the middle of our unhealthy mourning, we caught ourselves— something needed to be done to change our outlook on the tragedy of losing him. We reached out to Cami, Josh's widow, a person we might have easily chosen to distance ourselves from in order to shut out the pain of loss. Truthfully, we didn't know the right things to say or do, so we simply decided to show up and listen. We realized that this might be uncomfortable for us, but it was nothing in comparison to what she was going through.

So one evening, Cami, her sister, Tina, and the two of us sat around a table together. As dusk began to settle, we started speaking openly about Josh. None of us anticipated how the conversation would go. Tears were shed as we sat there, the dark falling around us, but it was our way of stepping into our loss and accepting it.

When we made the decision to have that conversation about Josh, we knew what might be at stake. Confronting our loss wasn't easy, but that moment came out of the intentional decision not to run away from thinking about Josh. What did we give up by engaging in Cami's friendship? We gave up what was easy—fantasizing and trying to deny his death altogether—and stepped into a place where we felt unsure. But that's where change is built: in the uneasiness and discomfort. And out of that, we built a great relationship with somebody who mattered more than anything in the world to Josh. And Cami now works with us as an executive assistant for our business.

Changing your situation is about not sidestepping the issue or avoiding the elephant in the room. It's about moving into uncertainty with openness and honesty, and realizing that this choice might bring with it anxiety, discomfort, and even pain. It's about being willing to accept what comes, about being vulnerable. By being open to this kind of honesty and vulnerability, you also open yourself to a sense of freedom, peace, and emotional richness that otherwise may never have entered your life.

You have the power to change your situation for the better, no matter what. But before you can do that, you may have to give up some of the stories, ideas, and assumptions you've been clinging to about yourself and your current situation. So when times are really tough, remind yourself that giving up doesn't always mean you're weak or wrong. Often, it simply means you're strong enough and smart enough to let go and move forward with your life.

With that in mind, here are a few key things to consider giving up if you want to empower yourself to embrace change and get unstuck from a situation that's holding you back.

Give Up the Excuses You Keep Reciting to Yourself

Because all the excuses and explanations in the world won't do you any good. They won't add any value to, or improve the quality of, your life in the slightest. To fulfill your present calling and get where you wish to go in life require more than just thinking and talking. These feats require focused and sustained action. And the good news is, you're perfectly capable of taking whatever action is necessary. You just have to choose to do it.

Sooner or later, you will realize that it's not what you lose along the way that counts; it's what you do with what you still have. When you let go of the past, forgive what needs forgiving, and move forward, you in no way change the past—you change the present and future.

Once You're over the Excuses, Give Up the Idea That You Don't Have What It Takes

You do have exactly what it takes. Will it be easy? Absolutely not! To paraphrase a quote from the infamous Rocky Balboa character, no one is going to blindside you and hit you as hard as life will. But it's not about how hard life can hit you; it's about how hard you can be hit while continuing to move forward. That's what true strength is. And that's what winning the game of life is all about.

In the end, all the small things make a big difference. Every step is crucial. Life isn't about a single moment of great triumph and attainment. It's about the trials and errors that slowly get you there—the blood, sweat, tears, and the small, inconsequential things you do on a day-to-day basis. It all matters in the end—every step, every regret, every decision, every minor setback and minuscule win.

The seemingly useless happenings add up to something. The minimum-wage job you had in high school. The evenings you spent socializing with coworkers you never see anymore. The hours you spent writing thoughts on a personal blog that no one reads. Contemplations about elaborate future plans that never came to be. All those lonely nights spent reading novels and news columns and comic strips, questioning your own principles on life and sex and religion and whether or not you're good enough just the way you are.

All of this has strengthened you. All of this has led you to every success you've ever had. All of this has made you who you are today. And all of this proves that you have the strength to deal with the challenges in front of you.

Give Up Focusing on What's Wrong, and Start Noticing What's Right

What you see often depends entirely on what you are looking for. Do your best and surrender the rest. When you stay stuck in regret about the life you think you should have had, you end up missing the beauty of what you actually do have. You will have a hard time ever being happy if you aren't thankful for the good things in your life right now.

You don't need ideal circumstances to move forward. The happiest and most successful people do not live with a certain set of circumstances, but rather with a certain set of attitudes. Choosing to be positive and grateful for what you have now is going to determine how you're going to live the rest of your life. So instead of waiting until everything is just right, look for something positive about today. Even if you have to look a little harder than usual, it still exists.

Give Up the Tendency to Get Caught Up in People's Harmful Judgments and Opinions

The biggest prison you will likely ever live in is fear of what other people think. You cannot let other people tell you who you are or what you want. You have to decide that for yourself. When you're making big decisions, remember, what you think of yourself and your life is more important than what people think of you. Don't let others make you feel guilty for living *your* life. As long as you're not hurting anyone else, live it *your* way.

It's okay to listen to others sometimes, but not at the expense of your own authenticity or sanity. Throughout your life, there will be many times when everything gets really quiet and the only thing left is the echoing pulse of your own intuition. Learn to recognize what it sounds like, or you'll never understand what it's telling you.

Be ready to stand up for what you stand for!

And remember that no matter how much determination and willpower you have, if you keep yourself in a relationship or social environment that works against your best intentions, you may eventually succumb to that environment. (We'll cover this in detail in chapter 9.)

Give Up Procrastinating and Senselessly Wasting Time

To make this point, we'll paraphrase a quote we've always loved by Marc Levy, from his novel *If Only It Were True:* You are the customer of a bank called Time. Every morning, it credits you with 86,400 seconds. Every night it writes off, as a loss, whatever remainder you have failed to invest to good purpose. It carries over no balance. It allows no overdraft. Each day, it opens a new account for you with the same deposit of 86,400 seconds. Each night, it burns the remains of the day. If you fail to use the day's deposits, the loss is yours. There is no going back. There is no drawing against tomorrow.

Time is not a resource you can borrow or take from your

reserves whenever you need it; it's a constraint. You must live in the present on today's deposits only. Invest that time so you can get from it the utmost in health, happiness, and success. You're making withdrawals right this second, so make them count.

Finally, Give Up Choosing to Do Nothing

You don't get to choose how you are going to die or when. You can only decide how you are going to live right now. Every day is a new chance to choose. Choose to change your perspective. Choose to flip the switch in your mind from negative to positive. Choose to turn on the light and stop fretting with insecurity and doubt. Choose to do work that you are proud of. Choose to see the best in others, and to show your best to others. Choose to truly *live* your life right now.

When you stop doing the wrong things, you give the right things a chance to catch up with you. So take a moment to think about one bad habit or thought pattern that has been making you unhappy and keeping you stuck in your current situation, whether it's one of the items above or something else. What can you give up today that you can replace with something useful, something that will help you change your situation and get you back to happy?

Many of us suffer from a misalignment of our priorities. We fill our calendars, our social media feeds, and our days with various forms of distraction and busyness, often just to avoid doing the little things that must be done or being slightly uncomfortable with the workload in front of us. The instant we feel a bit of discomfort, we run off in the direction of the nearest shiny object that catches our attention. And this habit gradually dismantles our best intentions and our true potential. Our dreams and priorities go by the wayside, and we're left regretting another wasted day.

But it doesn't have to be this way.

We can choose differently.

We can embrace the changes we know we need to make.

In fact, embracing change of all kinds is the only viable option we have.

Why Embracing Change Is Crucial

Change is constant. There is no force strong enough to stop it. It's up to you to adapt to the ups and downs of life, but once you start to take action toward embracing change, you'll reap the benefits in ways you maybe didn't anticipate: You'll feel proud, because you're making progress. You'll feel relief, because you're finally moving forward. But most important, you'll feel the freedom that comes from taking those small steps.

The truth is, living is a risk. Happiness is a risk. If you're not a little scared sometimes, then you're not doing it right. Don't worry about mistakes and failures; worry about what you're giving up when you don't even try. Worry about the life you're not living and the opportunities you're forgoing by choosing to exist in the safety of your comfort zone. Give yourself permission to be one of the people who survived doing it wrong, who made mistakes but recovered from them and grew into their strongest self. That's what we wish for ourselves, and that's what we wish for you.

The road ahead is wide open. Here are some good reasons for all of us to embrace change and move forward.

Everything Changes, Whether
You Embrace Change or Not

Most of us are comfortable where we are, even though the whole universe is constantly changing around us. Learning to accept this is vital to our happiness and general success. Because only when we change do we grow and begin to see a world we never knew was possible. And don't forget, however good or bad a situation is now, it will change. That's the one thing you can count on. So embrace it, and steer into the change you want in your life. It won't always be easy or obvious at first, but in the end it will be worth it.

There's Plenty of Life Left to Be Lived

We get one shot at the present, and we can make it great. There's no age limit on changing your course, and to settle in and be stuck in a life that isn't authentic is a tragic waste. It's never too late or too early to become who you are capable of being. It's up to you, so make the best of it. Do things that startle you. Feel things you've never felt before. Spend time with people who help you grow. Live a life you're proud of. And if you find that you're not, find the courage to change things again.

You Can't Grow by Standing in One Place

> Sometimes you must let go to grow.

When things aren't adding up in your life, it's time to start subtracting. As we've mentioned, sometimes you must let go to grow. You cannot discover new oceans unless you build up enough courage to lose sight of the old, familiar shoreline. Be brave. Follow your values. Listen to your intuition. And remember, no venture is ever a waste of time. The ones that don't work out teach you lessons that prepare you for the ones that do.

The Past Never Changes

You can spend days, weeks, months, or even years sitting alone in a dark room, overthinking things, twisting everything around in your head, trying to make all the puzzle pieces fit, while suffocating yourself with the reasons everything didn't turn out like it was supposed to. Or you can just leave the pieces in the dark and walk out the front door into the sunlight to get some fresh air and take a step forward.

Holding On to Old Pain Is Self-Abuse

Your past has given you the strength and wisdom you have today, so celebrate it. Don't let it haunt you. Replaying a painful memory over and over in your head is a form of self-abuse. Toxic thoughts create a toxic life. Make peace with yourself and your past. When you heal your thoughts, you create a space where happiness can flourish. So stop focusing on old problems and things you don't want in your future. The more you think about them, the more you attract what you fear into your everyday experiences.

> Toxic thoughts create a toxic life.

Moving On Creates Positive Change

You may blame everyone else and think, "Poor me! Why do all these crappy things keep happening to me?" But the only thing those scenarios all have in common is *you*. And this is good news, because it means you alone have the power to change things, or at least change the way you think about things. There is something very powerful and liberating about surrendering to change and embracing it, for this is where personal growth and evolution reside.

New Opportunities Are Out There Waiting for You

Nobody gets through life without challenges and disruptions, just as nobody gets through life without losing someone they love, something they need, or something they thought was meant to be. But it is these trials that make us stronger and eventually move us toward future opportunities. Embrace these opportunities. Enter new relationships and new situations knowing that you are venturing into unfamiliar territory. Be ready to learn, be ready for a challenge, and be ready to experience something or meet someone that just might change your life forever.

Remember this: at the end of the day, you are your greatest asset. You have all the strength and determination you need inside you; you just have to tap into it to make the most of the change that's swirling all around you, just waiting to be harnessed to create something better.

Closing Exercise and How to Ignite Your Passion

As Nelson Mandela once said, "It always seems impossible until it is done."

Any goal you have might seem impossible when looked at as a whole. The trick is recognizing that it doesn't have to happen all at once. Small acts of positive intention will only help to strengthen your resolve, reignite your passion for living, and ultimately make it easier for you to turn your life for the better.

It's important to remember that no act of changing your situation will cause regression, as long as that act is positive and intentional. With this in mind, one simple thing to start with when things are getting stressful, and your passion for taking action is sapped, is to spend ten minutes taking a walk to clear your mind. A short walk does wonders. It gives you something new to look at, gets your body moving, and is a quick way to get yourself physically out of your present situation.

Through a decade of life coaching, we've found that people who have recently experienced stressful life events like a serious illness, the death of a loved one, marital separation, or job loss, and are struggling to cope, always see an immediate mood boost after a short outdoor walk, especially if it's in a park or green space. It's possibly the most effective way to instantly reduce the anxieties of a drained and worried mind.

As deceptively simple as taking a walk might be, you're taking actual steps toward changing something in your life you don't like. Those ten minutes of walking are proof that you have the power to change your situation, even if it just means moving from your chair and desk to the outdoors for a brief spell. Your short walk represents a small journey that can make a huge difference—it can help you inject a little bit of extra passion into the present moment. And that's a really big deal!

Let this little walk and renewed passion for the moment be a reminder that passion is not something you find in life; it's some-thing you do. When you want to find the passion and inner strength needed to change your situation, you have to force yourself to step forward.

Many of us are still hopelessly trying to "find our passion"—something we believe will ultimately lead us closer to happiness, success, or the life situation we ultimately want. And we say "hope-lessly" primarily because passion can't really be found. When we say we're trying to find our passion, it implies that our passion is somehow hiding behind a tree or under a rock somewhere. But that's far from the truth. The truth is, our passion comes from doing things right. If you're waiting to somehow "find your passion" somewhere outside yourself, so you finally have a reason to put your whole heart and soul into your life and the changes you need to make, you'll likely be waiting around for an eternity.

On the other hand, if you're tired of waiting, and you'd rather live more passionately starting today and experience small positive changes, it's time to proactively inject passion into the very next thing you do. Think about it:

- When was the last time you sat down and had a conversation with someone you love, with zero distractions and 100 percent focus?
- When was the last time you exercised and put every bit of effort you could muster into it?
- When was the last time you truly tried—*truly* tried— to do your very best?

Like most of us, you're likely putting a halfhearted effort into most of the things you do on a daily basis. Because you're still waiting. You're still waiting to "find" something to be passionate about—some magical reason to step into the life you want to create for yourself. But you need to do the exact opposite!

When Marc was a kid, his grandmother used to tell him, "Stop waiting for better opportunities. The one you have in front of you is the best opportunity." She also said, "Too often we spend too much time making it perfect in our heads before we ever even do it. Stop waiting for perfection and just do your best with what you have today, and then improve it tomorrow."

Believe it or not, recent psychological research indirectly reinforces Marc's grandmother's sentiments. For many years, psychologists believed our minds could directly affect our physical state of being, but never the other way around. Nowadays, however, it is widely documented that our bodies—for example, our momentary facial expressions and body posture—can directly affect our mental state of being too. So while it's true that we change from the inside out, we also change from the outside in. And you can make this reality work for you. If you want more passion in your life right now, act accordingly right now.

Take a short walk and then put your heart and soul into something!

Not into tomorrow's opportunities, but into the opportunity right in front of you.

Not into tomorrow's tasks, but into today's tasks.

Not into tomorrow's run, but into today's run.

Not into tomorrow's relationships, but into today's relationships.

We are certain you have plenty in your life right now that's worth your time and energy. You have people and circumstances in your life that need you as much as you need them. You have a massive reservoir of potential passion within you, just waiting. Put your heart and soul into what you've got right in front of you. Your long-lost passion will show up to greet you. And your situation will start to change for the better.

CHAPTER 7

Motivation: Harness Your Inner Drive and Keep Moving Forward

Embrace your why, get going, then keep going.

t's been over a decade since we began the blog that would eventually become *Marc & Angel Hack Life*. At the time, we had no idea how to design a website. We barely even knew what a blog was. All we knew was that we were passionate about writing and needed an outlet. We had things that we wanted to say, people we wanted to reach, but we weren't sure how to begin.

Our friend had died a week prior (a different friend). We were huddled around the kitchen table, contemplating this loss and struggling with the concept of beginning something we'd always wanted to do. In college, we'd thought about blogging, especially as we mulled over the ideas we'd been taught in our psychology courses. At that time, we felt as though there were a hundred blogs dedicated to self-improvement. What could we say that would be any different?

At that table, we considered that we were experiencing some of the psychological issues we'd learned years before, and that we were once again second-guessing ourselves. Our negative thoughts were the biggest enemy, forcing us to doubt ourselves and convince us that our ideas and words weren't good enough.

So we started the blog. We learned the ins and outs gradually, making mistakes along the way. At first, it was just our family and friends reading our articles. One month, we wrote several posts about our personal struggles with loss, and these amassed more readers. Then, sadly, we were faced with a period of even deeper loss. So we continued to write about our losses, our sadness, and how we were struggling to grow through it all. Before we knew it, our small-time blog was being read by hundreds, and then thousands, of people every day. People were connecting with us, and we in turn were connecting with them. We were giving them hope, and they were in turn giving us hope. And that was just the beginning of a beautiful, decade-long journey that's still going strong.

It was frightening to start something we'd never done before. It was difficult to put ourselves out there, especially with the negative voices chattering away in our heads, telling us we couldn't or shouldn't do it, that we couldn't handle telling our stories, that we weren't ready yet. But a powerful thing happened when we started blogging even before we felt ready. We discovered new ways of achieving what had once seemed out of reach. We healed our broken hearts. We developed our own voices. We developed our own writing style. We connected with thousands of amazing people around the world. And by focusing not on the reasons we should stop, but on the reasons we should continue, our blog got better and better. Today, more than three million people read it every month.

We could have easily listened to the negative voices. We could have delayed once again, simply because it was simpler to listen to the lies we were telling ourselves than it was to summon the motivation needed to take the plunge.

Motivation isn't always an easy thing to come by, especially in tough times. Life has ways of throwing up barriers that keep us from making progress toward the goals and ideas that matter the most. And so often we lose or lack motivation simply by getting in our own way! But thankfully, motivation can be cultivated in many ways as well. In this chapter, we'd like to share with you several powerful ways in which you can cultivate and harness your own inner motivation, so you have the drive to take the daily steps forward that you know you are meant to take.

What Is Motivation?

At its most basic level, motivation is what spurs you to act on a desire; it's the determination and drive to make that desire a reality. Motivation moves you to show up to the project and get the right things done. It's the force that moves an idea from point A—where it lives only in your head—to point B—where you make the idea a reality.

There are two big pieces to motivation: the motivation to *just get started*, and the motivation to *keep going*. In the best of worlds, one leads to the other: once you find the motivation to get started, your progress keeps you going as you build and sustain momentum. For example, let's say you want to write a book. You begin by writing every day, perhaps even just five hundred words a day to start. And with every passing day, you begin to see the book take form, more and more words turning into chapters and sections. As you see what you're creating start to take shape, the momentum begins to pile up too. Then suddenly you find that you've written the whole thing!

But in the real world, this is often easier said than done. So often, we start a new project only to fall off the bandwagon a few days later. Inertia and fear creep in, and the desire for an easy way out dominates our desire to see our idea become a reality.

We're here to keep you from falling into this trap—to give you some tools for your arsenal, strategies to fall back on when the lazy days threaten to swallow your motivation whole. In these next few sections, we're going to provide you with several tested methods that will help you jump-start your motivation.

Get Motivated by Having a Powerful *Why*

If you're like us, you can motivate yourself to do just about any small task. But when it comes to accomplishing a larger goal, you often need some serious willpower, and willpower is best achieved by having a great *why*. A great *why* is your meaningful connection to your goal, and it's what will ultimately be your saving grace, the thing you fall back on when all else fails.

Your *why* is found simply by asking yourself: Why am I doing this? What's the big reason behind my desire to accomplish it? When we can connect to our goal and see the bigger picture, it's much easier to *want* to accomplish that goal. For instance, think about the common goal of getting in shape. To say you want to get back in shape because you want to be healthy is a good start, but it's not the *why* that's going to dig you out of a hole when you've lost your motivation. You need to look a little deeper to uncover what's really behind that reason. Being healthier is a good goal, but why specifically do you want to be healthier?

When we asked ourselves this exact question, it came down to how we visualized our lives and what we wanted to see in the future. We wanted to be healthy because we hoped for a long life in which we could see our child raise his own children—we realized we wanted to be grandparents someday and experience everything in between. Now that's a powerful *why*.

When your *why* is substantial and meaningful, you have an automatic, built-in source of powerful motivation. When you set yourself an ambitious goal, you're going to encounter many times when you won't feel the motivation to do the things you need to in order to achieve that goal. In those moments, checking in with your *why* can help you reset your priorities and rekindle the motivation to move forward.

Once you've established your *why*, your chosen pursuit takes on a powerful meaning. Knowing that your goal is something worthwhile will help you stay on track when your dedication is flagging. Now that you've got this bedrock principle in place, we're going to show you a few more ways to cultivate the motivation to move toward your goals and make them reality.

Get Motivated by Eliminating Distractions

There are many ways to motivate yourself to achieve your goal, all of which may differ for each individual. But one time-tested motivational method of ours is to eliminate as many distractions as possible.

Distractions are easily defined as tasks not directly related to achieving your *why*. Again, your *why* comes in very handy here, because it can help you determine what is or isn't a distraction. Once you've identified *why* you're doing something, then it's much easier to identify whether or not you're focusing on the *right* tasks.

For example, if your goal is to finish writing a book, you wouldn't want to fill up your day with tasks that are irrelevant to your project. You don't want to have other distractors lurking nearby—the email in-box or the social media feed—that can take your focus away from the one task with a meaningful connection to your goal: writing.

In order to make sure we know what our distractions are ahead of time, we sit down every evening and plan for the day ahead, writing out what needs to get done. There's a deliberateness to this list, because we're asking ourselves *why* those things need to be done. We're crossing off the things that distract us from our real needs and/or goals.

We take the time to do this mainly because it's easy to do the things that don't matter. Not everything you do in life will be fun and exciting, but when you can identify the *why*—or lack thereof—behind each of your to-do items, it becomes much easier to eliminate the fun, easy distractions that are setting you back. Then you can look at what remains on your list and ask yourself: What's here that I don't need to do? What's here that's just getting in the way of my accomplishing the right work? What am I doing just to stay busy?

Remind yourself that you become a true master of your life when you learn how to master your focus—where your attention goes. Value what you give your energy to. Do your best to let go of all the purposeless clutter, drama, and aimless time wasting that keeps getting in your way. It's time to focus on what matters!

Again, this is easier said than done, and busywork can *feel* productive. Before you know it, you might find you've spent an entire day on small, generally meaningless tasks. But why does this happen? Why is it always easier to do the little, unimportant things? Because they don't require as much ownership. The things that matter simply require more of you. More of your time, your thoughts, your energy, *you*. Thankfully, your meaningful connection to your goal—your *why*—is your way through this predicament, giving you the motivation to eliminate the distractions and pay attention to what matters, and to do the things that will help you grow and move in the right direction.

Get Motivated by Tracking Your Progress

A crucial step in setting any goal is to break it down into small, achievable steps. This is another valuable way to stay motivated, but it's easy to miss the importance of measuring and tracking your progress and success. Truth is, this is a simple strategy that can pay huge dividends! Simply by taking a look at what you've achieved in a given day, and comparing it to where you were the day before, you can see your tangible progress and use it as fuel to motivate you further.

If you have a multipart project that has to get done, seeing it come together slowly might seem discouraging. But if you look at where you started and compare it to where you are now, you'll see how far you've come. It might not be exactly where you want to be ultimately, but seeing that progress will help motivate you to take the next step, and the next.

When it comes to tracking your progress, try to set up lots of mini milestones along the way. Every small step counts! We did this in a big way when we were revamping our blog. As our readership grew, we knew we needed to make the interface look more professional. Rather than attempt to overhaul it all at once, we focused on making gradual changes and tracking our progress. First, we made the interface look a little cleaner. Then we focused on properly organizing and archiving our past articles. And with each new step, we'd take time to reflect and measure our progress. We noticed what was succeeding and what was not.

No matter what you're trying to achieve, tracking and noticing your progress is like setting up "mile markers" on your route to happiness and success. We tend to smile when we see proof of ourselves moving forward. But remember not to fall into the trap of comparing your progress with that of others—we all need our own time to travel our own distance. Just focus on the step you are taking, and measure your progress against your previous step.

Use Hardship as a Springboard

On a sunny April morning six years ago, Angel rolled her ankle and tore all the ligaments and tendons in her foot. She couldn't walk for ten weeks. She experienced a lot of negativity as a result of this accident, including the sudden inability to do many of the things she could do physically before the accident. But she also experienced the exciting possibilities that can come about when one is faced with adversity. In fact, not being able to walk or run created a whirlwind of motivation for Angel.

After the initial dismay of the accident wore off, Angel began to consider that there were many other people in worse positions than hers, some of whom would perhaps never be able to walk again. Although she would need time to heal and recover, she also knew she would most likely have the opportunity and the ability to use her legs again before long. But she still wondered why would she risk wasting this opportunity, this gift of being able to recover?

So she used the accident as a springboard to set an audacious goal, and challenged herself to run a half marathon.

By setting this goal, she had established a powerful *why*: she would recover so she could run the half marathon. First came physical therapy to get her back on her feet, then powerwalking a mile twice a day until she built up the strength to run again. Once she was able to run, she created a system to track her progress. Her goal for the half marathon was to run the entire way. So she set up a running schedule. First it was two miles per day, then the next week three miles per day, and so on, until she could run ten miles straight. Every week, she would build on the progress of the week before. She was combining motivational strategies—finding her *why,* overcoming hardship, and tracking her progress—to help maximize her chances of succeeding.

In chapter 5, we talked about the idea of post-traumatic growth, how hardships and traumas can lead to powerful creative and intellectual development. When we run into adversity—whether it's physical damage to our bodies, the loss of a job, or something else—our initial reaction may be to mourn, and even to become depressed. But when framed and leveraged the right way, our setbacks and traumas can help motivate us, making us emotionally stronger, more resourceful, and ultimately happier.

We need to remember that all of us can heal through hardships, and many of us are even catapulted onto a more meaningful, motivated path after experiencing one. Growth through hard times is far more common than most of us realize. The challenge is to bring awareness to the opportunity presented by these kinds of unexpected and undesirable events. Afterward, we need hope. In the aftermath of intense pain, we need to know there is something better—and there almost always is. A traumatic experience is not simply a painful experience to be endured. Instead, it can be incredibly life changing by motivating us to evolve in the best ways possible.

It isn't an easy journey, but most of us have the mental and emotional capacity to emerge from our hardships—even severe ones—stronger, more focused, and with a better perspective on life. In numerous psychological studies of people who have suffered traumatic hardships, about 50 percent of them report positive changes in their lives as a result of their negative experiences. Some changes are small (more appreciation for the average day, for example), while others are so seismic that they propel them onto totally new and rewarding life paths. The bottom line is that the most painful things that could possibly happen to us *can* be pivotal circumstances of great opportunity. Hardships often push us to face the reality of life's impermanence, to appreciate our limits, and to find more meaningful understandings of who we are and how we want to spend the rest of our lives.

Angel's ankle accident pales in comparison to many of the hardships people face in this world, and even many of the other hardships we have faced. But in a situation like her accident, we can still use the power of post-traumatic growth to inspire us toward meaningful goals. We almost never willingly choose to be in pain or incapacitated. But using these situations to motivate us toward a bigger goal can help push us in directions we might never have thought to go before.

Get Motivated by Overcoming Scarcity

Right before our son was born, we had a goal to build a self-paced online teaching course—based on ten years of extensive one-on-one and two-on-one coaching experience with our clients. We knew the course would be an invaluable resource to those who needed coaching assistance but also wanted to work at their own pace. Our barrier? Building a valuable online teaching resource like this takes a lot of focus and effort. So it was constantly on the back burner—until we found out we were pregnant and no longer had what felt like an infinite amount of time to accomplish our goal. We knew our time would be scarce when Mac was born, which in turn made our time more important. So we set the deadlines, and got it done. The simple fact that we had a deadline—the course had to be finished before his birth—made us finally accomplish that goal.

Once you start to experience a scarcity of some kind, it's amazing how quickly you can become motivated. Scarcity is a handy motivator, and time is one of the most "usefully scarce" resources in the world. Time scarcity is used as a powerful motivational strategy in many contexts, including on popular social networks like Snapchat and Instagram. These platforms let you create "stories"—sequences of pictures and videos—that are designed to exist for only twenty-four hours. If you miss a story, it will disappear and you'll never see it again. This causes people to stay glued to their devices constantly, reflexively checking for updates.

This example shows how scarcity is a motivational power that can be used in arguably negative ways—but it can also be leveraged to your advantage if you use it carefully and thoughtfully. We always wish we had more time, and when it's threatening to vanish, we often suddenly realize just how important it is. So use that moment of realization to jolt you into action! Setting yourself a deadline and deciding that your goal is *meant* to be done in a specific time frame will greatly improve your ability to accomplish it and stay motivated.

Get Motivated by Being SMART

We may never have realized the motivational power of overcoming scarcity had we not been introduced to SMART goals. This is a simple tool we've used for years to help set goals that make sense, and to motivate ourselves to accomplish them. SMART stands for specific, measurable, attainable, relevant, and timely. Let's briefly review what each of these elements means:

- **Specific**: A specific goal has a far greater chance of being accomplished because it has defined parameters and constraints.
- **Measurable**: When you measure your progress, you stay on track, reach your target dates, and experience the exhilaration of achievement that spurs you on to continued efforts required to reach your goal.
- **Attainable**: To be attainable, a goal must represent an objective toward which you are both willing and able to work. In other words, the goal must be realistic. The big question here is: *how* can the goal be accomplished?
- **Relevant**: Relevance stresses the importance of choosing goals that matter. For example, an internet entrepreneur's goal to make seventy-five tuna sandwiches by 2:00 p.m. may be specific, measurable, attainable, and timely, but it lacks relevance to an entrepreneur's overarching objective of building a profitable online business.
- **Timely**: A goal must be grounded within a time frame, giving the goal a target date. A commitment

to a deadline helps you focus your efforts on
the completion of the goal on or before the due date.

Making sure all of your goals are SMART makes it immensely more likely that you'll succeed. So if you're struggling to make progress toward a goal, ask yourself: *am I being SMART about this?*

Get Motivated with Rewards and Consequences

Another powerful set of motivators are rewards and consequences. Think of them as the *good cop–bad cop* system of motivation: you can choose to reward yourself for completing a task, or face a not-so-fun consequence if you don't. You can use these strategies together or separately; the key is to figure out which combination will best motivate you—a reward, a consequence, or both.

Rewards-based motivation is pretty straightforward. If you finish your assigned tasks in a certain time frame, you can then reward yourself with something you enjoy that you might not normally do during the day. For us, we like to make sure the reward itself is a rare treat that will disappear based on time. If we get all of our work done, we'll often use watching a movie with our son as a reward. Spending time with our son and simply relaxing is an enormous motivator; it works every time. You might use TV as a reward too, watching the latest episode of your favorite show as a reward for completing a specific task. It's up to you what you choose as a reward, as long as it's something you'll truly look forward to.

On the other end of the spectrum is consequence-based motivation, a method that our clients have also used with success. If something negative is definitely going to happen as a consequence of not completing your task, you have a pretty motivating reason to get it done. As humans, we're actually wired to experience losses more negatively than we experience gains positively, a phenomenon called *loss aversion*. Studies have shown, for instance, that most people are far more motivated to avoid losing a hundred dollars than they are to earn a hundred dollars.

But you can use this tendency to your advantage by turning it into a form of motivation. So decide, for instance, that if you don't meet your goal in the allotted time, then you'll have to donate one hundred dollars to a charity of your choosing. Better yet, for even more motivation, decide that you'll donate that money to a charity whose aims you *don't* agree with. When we add the risk of losing money *and* doing something that goes against our views and preferences, most of us will get moving!

Get Motivated with Accountability

We've discussed accountability in previous chapters, but it's also incredibly important when it comes to getting and staying motivated. In chapter 1, we talked about not breaking the chain—tracking your progress on a chart each day, making sure not to break the line of progress markers—as a way to stick to your rituals. By deciding that you won't break the chain, you're holding yourself accountable for your progress using a tangible visual cue—for example, looking at your desk calendar and seeing two weeks' worth of Xs marking your progress.

Visual reminders like this can be useful if you're the only one holding yourself accountable for your progress. But it can also help to have someone else play that role—an accountability partner. Having a partner, someone else who can check in on your progress and hold your feet to the fire, has been proven time and again to be a useful motivational tactic. In several studies, two groups of people were given the same set of tasks, and the group that was regularly checked up on was found to be more successful.

You can also "stack" accountability with consequences for extra motivation. For instance, you can set up rules and stipulations with your accountability partner to follow through on if you don't meet your goal. One simple way to do this is to agree that you'll give your partner a certain amount of money if you fail, or have your partner donate the money to that charity you don't agree with. That way, you're triple stacking yourself for success!

When Motivation Fails, Rely on Your Rituals

Remind yourself that you can't lift a thousand pounds all at once, but you can easily lift one pound a thousand times. Small, repeated, incremental efforts will get you there. It won't happen in an instant, but it will happen gradually, and it's something we've talked a lot about so far in this book: the power of rituals.

Remember what we discussed in chapter 1: goals don't make positive changes happen, daily rituals do. Too often we obsess over a goal—a result—but are completely unfocused when it comes to the ritual—the recurring steps—that ultimately make the goal happen. And so the weight of this unrealized goal sits heavy on our shoulders, and it slows us down to a crawl.

The key again is to keep it small; small rituals are easier to start and maintain. Making a big change all at once requires not only lots of grit and determination, but also lots of time and energy. And remember that small, incremental changes can add up to huge changes a lot faster than not getting there at all.

To dive back into the power of rituals, reread chapter 1.

Seven More Reminders to Help You Stay Motivated

At the end of the day, we know how difficult it can be to maintain our motivation. It's okay to feel frustrated, and it's normal to want to see results straightaway. Unfortunately, we don't get everything we want in life—at least, not unless we're willing to work for it! When you're feeling discouraged or defeated, here are seven helpful ideas to help you push through and rediscover your motivation.

1. **You are not the center of the universe—so stop making it all about *you*.**

    We all have the tendency to put ourselves at the center of the universe, and see everything from the viewpoint of how it affects us. But this can have many adverse effects, from feeling sorry for ourselves when things aren't going exactly as planned to doubting ourselves when we aren't perfect.

    Finding little ways to help others gets us out of self-centered thinking, so we're no longer wallowing in self-pity but are instead starting to think about what others need. We aren't doubting ourselves, because the question of whether we're good enough is no longer the central question. The central question now is about what others need. Thus, thinking about others instead of ourselves can help resolve our feelings of discouragement and defeat.

2. **It is your resistance to what is that causes your suffering—so be present.**

Happiness is allowing yourself to be perfectly okay with *what is* rather than wishing for and worrying about what is not. The rest is just you arguing with life. This means your suffering only ever occurs when you resist how things are in the present. Although you can't control everything that happens to you, you *can* control the way you respond to what happens. Your power is in your response to the situation. Your power is in your presence and acceptance.

3. **You are more than one thing—so loosen up and stretch your identity.**

We all have this picture in our minds of ourselves, this idea of what kind of person we are. When this idea gets threatened, we react defensively. Perhaps your identity for yourself is someone who's motivated and productive and has great ideas. But then when you're not motivated and not productive, you might feel defeated because you're worrying that you weren't who you thought you were. The solution is to realize that you're not just one thing. Sometimes you're productive, sometimes you're unproductive. Sometimes you're motivated, other times you feel lazy. You can be many things, and remembering this helps stretch your identity so it isn't so fragile. You make mistakes. You are less than perfect. And that's perfectly okay.

4. **Today is still a priceless gift—so make the best of it.**

You only have so many days left on Earth. Know that each one of those limited days is a gift, a blessing . . . a miracle. So we remind ourselves every morning that this day counts and that we need to make the best of it, even when times are tough. That doesn't mean we need to be hyperproductive or work ourselves into the ground, but that we should do something worthwhile to make the most of our time.

5. **Complaining is only making matters worse—so find a solution.**

    You will never get where you want to be by complaining about where you are now. We all have limited time and energy. Any time we spend whining is unlikely to help us achieve anything worthwhile. And it won't make us any happier either. If you took 10 percent of the energy you put into complaining and applied it to solving your present problems, you'd be surprised by how well and how quickly things can work out. When you stop complaining, and refuse to see yourself as a helpless victim, you'll find that you are far more powerful than you realized.

6. **Feeling discouraged and defeated is a sign that it's time to make a change—so make that change.**

    It could be a change of heart, a change in your perspective, or a change in your rituals. But the point in any case is that the way you are doing things is no longer working. When we feel discouraged and defeated, typically our first instinct is to look outside of ourselves for someone or something to blame. In reality, we ought to be looking at how we're feeling, what we're thinking, and how we plan to respond. Your life is your responsibility. And when you change the way you look at things, the things themselves change, which paves the way for positive action.

7. **Even the tiniest possible step is progress—so take a tiny step *now*.**

It can be hard to get moving when you're seriously stuck. You might have just lost your job or suffered through the loss of a loved one. Maybe you simply think your life isn't moving in the direction you wish it were, and you feel trapped.

This is how Marc felt a decade ago when he was stuck in a rut after simultaneously losing two loved ones to illness, then his family's financial stability. It was really hard to motivate himself when he didn't think he had the strength to push forward, when he felt insanely horrible and sorry for himself. But he took one tiny step every day—one journal entry, one workout, one honest conversation, and so forth—and it felt good, and he got stronger.

And believe it or not, that's basically what Marc did again this morning too. He was struggling to motivate himself after a significant business opportunity fell through. In Marc's words: *I was feeling discouraged and defeated, to say the least. But I knew I had work to do. So I took the tiniest possible step. Just turning on my computer, opening up the word processing application, and writing a single sentence. Such an action is so small as to seem insignificant, and yet so easy as to be possible when I was feeling utterly defeated. And it showed me the next step was possible, and the next. And the result is this small section of the chapter you're reading now.*

If you're finding yourself in a similar predicament, you can do the same thing—just take the tiniest possible step.

Take one deep, relaxing breath. Have one small glass of water and notice how it refreshes you—and reminds you that it's always possible to take a step in the right direction, however small, right now.

An Open Letter to Those Who Have Lost Their Motivation

We've covered a lot of ground already in this chapter, but we want to leave you with another open letter we wrote recently that was inspired by a short email we received from one of our newest course students:

> Dear Marc and Angel,
>
> There's so much I still want to create and foster in my life, and yet I feel utterly beaten down. I feel like I have nothing left to work with. I've been through a lot on my journey thus far, and I'm now at a point where I've lost all my motivation—I just can't seem to find the external and internal sources of motivation I used to have. Do you have any wisdom you could share?
>
> Sincerely,
>
> A Discouraged Student

Our reply (an open reply to all who have lost their motivation):

> Dear Discouraged Student,
>
> It's time for a quick story about life . . .
>
> Once upon a time there was a woman in her midsixties who noticed that she had lived her entire life in the same small town. And although she had spent decades enthusiastically dreaming

about traveling and seeing the world, she had never taken a single step to make this dream a reality.

Finally, she woke up on the morning of her sixty-fifth birthday and decided that now was the time! She sold all of her possessions except for some essential items she needed, packed these items into a backpack, and began her journey out into the world. The first several days on the road were amazing and filled with awe—with every step forward she felt like she was finally living the life she had dreamed.

But a few short weeks later, the days on the road started taking a toll on her. She felt misplaced, and she missed the familiar comforts of her old life. As her feet and legs grew more and more sore with each new step, her mood also took a turn for the worse.

Eventually she stopped walking, took off her backpack, slammed it on the ground, and sat down beside it as tears began streaming down her cheeks. She stared hopelessly down a long, winding road that once led to an amazing world, but now seemed to lead only to discomfort and unhappiness. "I have nothing! I have nothing left in my life!" she shouted out loud at the top of her lungs.

Coincidentally, a renowned guru and life adviser from a nearby village was resting quietly behind a pine tree adjacent to where the woman was sitting. As the woman was shouting, the guru heard every word and felt it was his duty to help her. Without thinking twice, he jumped out from behind the pine tree, grabbed her backpack, and ran into the forest that lined both sides of the road. Stunned and in disbelief, the woman started crying even harder than before, to the point of near breathlessness.

"That backpack was all I had," she cried. "And now it's gone! Now everything is gone in my life!"

After ten minutes of much-needed tears, the woman gradually collected her emotions, stood up again, and began staggering slowly down the road. Meanwhile, the guru cut through the forest and secretly placed the backpack in the middle of the road just a short distance ahead of the woman.

When the woman's teary eyes fell upon the backpack, she almost couldn't believe what she was seeing—everything she thought she had just lost was once again right in front of her. She couldn't help but smile broadly. "Oh thank heavens!" the woman exclaimed. "I am so grateful! Now I definitely have what I need to continue onward . . ."

Remember, as we journey through our personal and professional lives, there will inevitably be periods of incredible frustration and despair. During those tough times, it will sometimes appear to us that we've lost everything, and that nothing and nobody could possibly motivate us to move onward in the direction of our dreams. But just like the woman who stumbled across the guru, we are all holding with us a backpack of support that comes in many forms—it can be a simple email or text message from someone we respect, inspiring blog posts, insightful books, helpful neighbors, tangible reminders, and so much more.

When we are feeling discouraged and unmotivated, our opportunity is twofold:

- To recognize and appreciate our backpack of support—our external sources of motivation—before a random guru (or someone with far more crooked intentions) has to steal it from us so that we can finally see what we have always taken for granted.

- To be present and tap into our own hearts and minds—our internal sources of motivation—which have the power to push us back up on our feet and guide us down the road to our backpack of support, even when it appears to be lost forever.

No matter your circumstances, you always have what you need to take the next smallest step. As Epicurus so profoundly said, "Do not spoil what you have by desiring what you have not; remember that what you now have was once among the things you only hoped for."

Be mindful. Be present. Keep going. One small step at a time.

Sincerely,

Marc and Angel

Closing Exercise

As we've discussed in this chapter, few good things come easily, and when the going gets tough, we often take the easy way out, even though the easy way usually takes us the wrong way. To combat this, successful people create tangible reminders that pull them back from the brink of their weak impulses. You may remember our friend from chapter 1 who motivated himself to pay off a ton of credit card debt by taping a copy of his credit card balance to his computer monitor. Or the other friend who keeps a photo of her heavier self on the refrigerator for motivation to stay healthy. Or the one who keeps a stack of family photos in his desk drawer to help him stay focused on what's important when work gets really tough.

Think of moments when you are most likely to give in to

impulses that sap your motivation and take you further from your ultimate goals. Then use visual reminders of those goals to interrupt the impulse and keep you on track. Here are a few examples:

- If you know you're prone to checking your phone when you should be staying on task, put a sticky note on top of it, marked with a giant X.
- If you're trying to write a book and find your mind wandering during your writing time, have a bulletin board next to you tacked with clippings and quotations that remind you of what your book is all about—and why you wanted to start it in the first place!
- If you're trying to eat healthier, put a calendar on your fridge. Mark each day you've continued to eat healthy—for your mind and your body—with a star. You'll see that reminder and know you have the power to continue.

CHAPTER 8

Relationships: Foster the Loving Connections You Deserve

One of the biggest gifts we can give ourselves is to foster the relationships that matter.

Marc grew up as an only child. His parents were professionals with impressive careers. His father held two master's degrees, one in education and one in business, and his mother was a psychiatric nurse for children.

Yet when he was younger, Marc realized that his parents had started to let their relationship go, ignoring it while their careers flourished. It was remarkable to Marc that two intelligent and loving human beings could become so obsessive about their careers that they would forget to take time to foster their relationship with each other.

Most important, however, is when the arguments in the household were hitting their peak, Marc's parents recognized the problem and both made a commitment to fix it. It can be difficult to accept that you're on a path you hadn't anticipated. And Marc's parents are no different from most. They both made a sincere commitment to each other, and along the way, life got hectic, mistakes were made, priorities got skewed, and unintentional neglect flooded in. But they were willing to put in the necessary effort to make the relationship work and heal the broken pieces.

That's where therapy came in. In a relatively short time, his parents were able to resolve their differences and start seeing eye to eye. They're still happily married today, and their relationship is stronger than ever. It's not that their relationship was ever bad, but they simply lost track of each other in the mix of everything else that happens in life. Seeing his parents struggle made Marc realize how a relationship can easily start to go the wrong way—but it also helped him see how it can be healed if the people involved are willing to work on it.

It can be difficult to realize that a relationship does in fact need work. In our closest relationships, we long for honesty and strength. Yet we convince ourselves that these relationships are always going to be there for us, no matter what. And that's where neglect trickles in. We start to take these relationships for granted. We get involved with other passions. We don't have time for everything, and something inevitably has to give. Unfortunately, sometimes—or often—what ends up giving way is what matters most: our connection to the people we love the most.

The Hard Truths About Our Relationships No One Wants to Admit

We all long for authentic relationships, but they can be hard to find, even in our overly connected lives. We meet people in person and socialize online, but these connections often lack a necessary dose of intimacy. We work alongside others in crowded office buildings, but our communication with them is usually work oriented and not relationship oriented. We may be lucky enough to have friends and family in our lives, but when we are distracted by social media and busy with work, those relationships take a hit.

So what does it take to create and nurture authentic relationships? That's a question we help our course students and coaching clients answer on a daily basis. After a decade of coaching individuals and couples and researching how people build authentic relationships, we've learned a lot about what it takes, and we've also learned a lot about the mistakes people make in the process. Recognizing these mistakes is half the battle, and once you see them for what they are, you're going to be better able to foster the sort of loving relationships you deserve.

One of the biggest mistakes we make is denying the truth about how we're acting in our relationships—how condescending we are; how unavailable we are; how little effort we put into them. But the good news is, we can change. Right here, right now, we can start by acknowledging some hard truths about our relationships.

Our relationships are filled with unnecessary judgments. When we judge, we learn nothing. Open your mind and heart. Don't judge people just because they behave differently than you. The world is changed by your example, not by your judgments. Remind yourself to be kind. To ask about people's feelings and stories. To listen. To be humble. To be open. Be a good friend and neighbor.

We look down on people when we disagree with them. When someone upsets you, it's often because they aren't behaving according to your fantasy of how they "should" behave. Take a deep breath. It's okay to disagree with the opinions of others, but that doesn't give you the right to deny any sense they might make. Nor does it give you the right to accuse them of lying just because you don't agree with them. Learn to appreciate different perspectives, life-styles, and opinions, even if it means overcoming your pride and opening your mind beyond what's initially com-fortable.

We tend to dwell on people's weaknesses. Be present. Be compassionate. Compliment people. Magnify their strengths, not their weaknesses. This is the simplest way to make a real and lasting difference in all your relationships.

There's a whole lot we don't know about the people in our lives. No matter how well you know someone, it's impos-sible to know exactly how another person is feeling or what kind of emotional battles they're fighting. Every smile or sign of strength hides an inner struggle every bit as complex and extraordinary as your own.

We carelessly gossip about our relationships. Don't give in to the unnecessary negativity, drama, and gossip around you. Be positive. Give people a piece of your heart rather than a piece of your mind. And listen carefully to how a person speaks to you about other people—this is precisely how they will speak about you to other people.

Our "busy" lives often get in the way of our most important relationships. The people you take for granted today may be the only ones you need tomorrow. Never be too busy to make time for the folks who matter most. Truly, the best gift you can give someone today is the purity of your undivided attention. Just be present with them, and pay attention.

We try to hide our flaws, even from those closest to us. As imperfect as you might be, as small as you sometimes feel, and as out of place as you imagine you are, you don't have to hide the flawed pieces of yourself. Remember, you attract other people to you by the qualities you show them, but you keep them around based on the qualities you truly possess. Personal flaws are a part of everyone's life. If you try to hide them, you don't give the people who care about you a chance to truly know and love the real you.

Our relationships aren't as easy as we want them to be. Good relationships require work, sacrifice, and compromise. They are amazing, but rarely easy. Resisting the hard times and seeing them as immediate evidence that something is wrong or that you're in the wrong relationship only aggravates the difficulties. In contrast, finding the willingness to view the challenges as opportunities to learn will give you the mind-set you need to bring your relationship to new heights.

We try to "fix" the people we care about. The act of sincerely caring for another person is rooted in love and respect. This means listening to them wholeheartedly and letting them know by your complete presence that they are seen, heard, and valued. It's not a space where you try to fix them—it's about being a witness to the beauty and totality of who they truly are.

We resist change within our relationships. Healthy, authentic relationships move in the direction of personal growth, for the relationship and for each person in it. Growth and change are a part of life, and you must embrace them. Even when you are concerned that a relationship may dissolve if things change, you must embrace the fact that your paths may diverge for all the right reasons.

Our failed relationships are far more important than we realize. Everyone has something important to teach you. Every relationship builds upon the lessons of those before it. Life doesn't always give you the people you want—it gives you the people you need, to learn, to grow, and then, eventually, to fall in love.

We take too many things too personally. There is a life-changing kind of inner freedom that comes to you when you detach yourself from other people's negative gestures and behaviors. The way others treat you is their issue; how you respond is yours. You know this. You simply can't take things too personally, even when it seems personal. Rarely do other people do things because of you—they do things because of them.

We like to get even with those who have wronged us. No matter how much someone seems to deserve it, nothing good ever comes from an act of revenge. Getting even doesn't help you get ahead. If you're feeling pain, don't take action that creates even more pain. Don't try to cover darkness with darkness. Find your light. Act out of love. Do something that will enable you to create a more fulfilling reality. Forgive. Let go of the resentment, learn from the incident, and move forward with your life, and hopefully you can move forward with your relationship too.

We are unknowingly in deep emotional relationships with anyone we hate. To hate someone is to hold on to them tightly—to cut out a lifelong space for them in your heart and mind. So let today be the day you stop allowing the ghosts of yesterday to haunt you. Let today be the day you stop poisoning yourself with hatred. Forget about getting even with those who have hurt you, and instead get even with those who have helped.

We are rarely as kind to others as we could be. All the hardest, coldest people you meet were once as innocent as a baby. And that's the tragedy of living. When people are rude, be your best—be kinder than necessary. No one has ever made themselves strong by showing how small or weak someone else is. Remember this, and communicate accordingly.

We place too much blame on our relationships. It's not anyone else's job to fill in your empty inner space. That's your job, and yours alone, and until you accept responsibility for your own emptiness and pain, your biggest problems will persist.

Reading through this list, you've likely identified with some of these points. You might also be wondering why it's so easy to get caught up in these types of behaviors. That's because, as we've said, fostering a healthy relationship can be hard work, and it's often easier to focus on the negatives rather than on the positives.

We have found that the best relationships are the best rarely because they have always been the happiest, but because they have stayed strong and resilient through the mightiest of storms. Over the years, we have worked with hundreds of individuals and couples looking to fix their failing relationships, and we've learned a lot about what it takes to make this happen.

Whether you're working to fix your marriage, a dating relationship, or a friendship, fortunately there are lots of things you can do to keep your relationships on track. This process starts by understanding exactly what makes a relationship a healthy one.

What Is a Healthy Relationship?

Now that we've learned the hard truths about how we often fall short in our relationships, let's talk about what healthy relationships look like and how you can start fostering them today. It's important to clarify that a healthy relationship includes not only intimate, romantic relationships, but also family relationships, friendships, and work relationships.

So what makes a relationship healthy? A healthy relationship is mutually beneficial, leaving you feeling renewed and fulfilled the majority of the time—you're getting something from the relationship, you're giving something to the relationship, and you want more of it all. It's a relationship in which you feel as though you can be yourself, in which you can be honest about your true feelings and grow as a person.

A healthy relationship is one where two people come into a space together and support each other honestly and openly. It's one in which they don't necessarily *need* each other, but their life is still better off with each other in it. Each person is mentally and emotionally strong enough to stand on their own two feet but can also lift the other up when the need arises.

In a healthy relationship, each person is meeting the other halfway. One person isn't doing all the taking while the other is doing all the giving. The caveat here is that human beings don't necessarily support each other fifty-fifty at all times. A healthy relationship has to be able to adapt to change. When one person can only give 20 percent, the other one needs to be willing to step up and give 80 percent. A healthy relationship is about giving a more when the other person can only give a little less.

Building this kind of relationship takes effort and intentionality, but it's not impossible. Take a few minutes now to acquaint yourself with some of the key qualities found in conscious, healthy relationships so you'll be better able to recognize and foster these behaviors for yourself.

The Seven Qualities of a Conscious, Loving Relationship

Over the past decade, between the two of us, we have read hundreds of books on relationships, coached hundreds of students and clients who were struggling to find happiness in their relationships, and interacted with thousands of readers who continue to ask us questions and tell us stories on a daily basis about their relationships. All of this has given us some insight into the behaviors and habits that make relationships work well in the long run. In our work, we often refer to these as the "qualities of conscious, loving relationships."

So what exactly is a conscious, loving relationship? It's a relationship, intimate or platonic, in which:

1. **Both people are emotionally self-reliant.**

    If your happiness is dependent on the constant validation and approval of someone else, then you are giving away far too much of your power. It's human nature to want to be liked and admired, to want to be included, but it's damaging to your self-esteem and emotional strength if it's something you have to constantly fight for.

The key is to nurture your own inner strength, then bring it into your relationships.

Think of a relationship as a home you live in. Whether you like your home or not doesn't depend on how the furniture is arranged—it's how you arrange your mind. You have to decide to love yourself in it, and then radiate this inner love outward.

All the love and validation you need is yours to give yourself. So the next time you feel pressured to impress someone, try taking a deep breath and reminding yourself that you don't owe anyone your constant justification. Revel in the reality that you get to choose. You have the authority to decide how to spend your time and energy. And here's the real beauty of it: when you don't owe anyone anything—when you're self-reliant—you're free to give and receive love from the heart, without baggage.

Come from this place of wholeness, of inner strength and independence, and then love others. Not because you need them to love you back, not because you're desperate to be needed, but because loving them is a miraculous thing to do.

2. **There's a solid foundation of mutual acceptance.**

Above all, acceptance means two people agree to disagree with each other on some things, and they're perfectly okay with it. Differences of opinion, even major ones, don't destroy relationships—it's how people in a relationship deal with their inevitable differences that counts.

Some friends and couples waste years trying to change each other's minds, but this can't always be done, because many of their disagreements are rooted in fundamental differences in how they see the world and themselves. By fighting over these deep-seated differences, all they succeed in doing is wasting their time and running their relationship into the ground.

So how do conscious, loving friends and couples cope with disagreements that can't be resolved? They accept one another as is—they understand that problems are an inevitable part of any long-term relationship, in the same way chronic physical difficulties are inevitable as we grow older and wiser. These problems are like a weak knee or a bad back—we may not want these problems, but we're able to cope with them, to avoid situations that irritate them, and to develop strategies that help us ease the pain. Psychologist Dan Wile said it best in his book *After the Honeymoon:* "When choosing a long-term partner or friend, you will inevitably be choosing a particular set of unsolvable problems that you'll be grappling with for the next 10, 20 or 50 years."

So just remember that the foundation of love is to let those we care about be unapologetically themselves, and not distort them to fit our own egotistical ideas of who they should be. Otherwise, we fall in love only with our own fantasies, and thus miss out entirely on their true beauty. Let this be your reality check. Instead of trying to change the people you care about, give them your support and grow together as individuals.

3. **Intentional communication is devotedly practiced.**

No one on this green earth is a mind reader. Share your thoughts openly. Give those you care about the information they need rather than expecting them to know it all. The more that remains unspoken, the greater the risk for problems. Start communicating as clearly as possible. Don't try to read anyone's mind, and don't make anyone try to read yours. Most problems, big and small, within a relationship start with broken communication.

Also, don't listen so you can reply—listen to understand. Open your ears and mind to people's concerns and opinions without judgment. Look at things from their perspective as well as your own. Try to put yourself in their shoes. Even if you don't understand exactly where they're coming from, you can still respect them. You can still put your phone away, turn your body toward them, and look them squarely in the eyes. Doing so demonstrates that you actually want to communicate and hear what they have to say. This reinforces the sort of supportive environment that's crucial for the growth of any relationship. (Later on in this chapter, we'll take a look at what happens when there's a communication breakdown.)

> **Listen to understand.**

4. **Disagreements are dealt with positively.**

When disagreements in a relationship arise, the easiest thing to do is to run away, especially if you're not a confrontational person by nature. But you have to catch yourself, because this isn't just about *you* and whether or not you feel like dealing with your differences. It's about what your relationship needs in order to grow and thrive in the long run. You have to put your relationship's needs ahead of your own for a moment. Both people must be committed to dealing with disagreements openly, because running from them will only make matters more difficult to deal with down the road.

One of the most simple and effective tools people in relationships can use to ease the process of dealing with disagreements is positive language. Relationships flourish when two people are able to share their innermost feelings and thoughts in a positive way. One effective method of doing this during a disagreement is to try your best to avoid using the word "you" and try to use the word "I" instead. This makes it much easier to express your true feelings while avoiding the possibility of verbally attacking the other person. So instead of saying, "You are wrong," try saying, "I don't understand." Instead of telling them, "You always . . . ," try saying, "I often feel . . ." It's a subtle shift that can make a big difference.

5. **Both people are allowed to save face.**

Marc's grandmother once told him, "When someone you love backs themselves into a corner, look the other way until they get themselves out, and then act as though it never happened." Allowing someone to save face in this way, and not reminding them of what they already know is not their most intelligent behavior, is an act of great kindness. This is possible when you realize that people typically behave in such ways because they are suffering momentarily. They react to their own thoughts and feelings, and their behavior often has nothing to do with you.

We all have unreasonable mood swings sometimes. We all have bad days. Giving your partner and friends the space to save face, and not taking things personally when they're occasionally upset, cranky, or having a bad day, is a priceless gift. Even if you are unquestionably right and they are unquestionably wrong, when emotions are flying high and you force them to lose face, you're simply bruising their heart and ego. You're accomplishing nothing but diminishing their worth in their own eyes.

Do your best to let the people in your life preserve their dignity. Give them space, let the emotions settle, and then have a rational conversation using the positive communication tactics discussed in the previous point.

6. **Personal growth is habitually sought and supported.**

You know how to tell if something is alive and well? You look for evidence of growth. Conscious, loving relationships contain two people who are committed to lifelong learning and growth. They're curious about things. They're keen to learn from the world and from each other. And because of their love for learning, they afford each other the freedom to develop as individuals within the relationship.

Throughout a decade of coaching our students and clients, we have seen many unhappy relationships that were caused primarily by one or both people being stubbornly clingy. In a nutshell, these "stubbornly clingy" people didn't want their friends or partners to change. But here's the simple truth: change is a part of the universe, and human beings are no exception. If you want to have a successful relationship, you've got to embrace personal growth with open arms, and all the changes that come with it.

7. **Love prevails.**

This final point encompasses the previous six, and then some. In a conscious, loving relationship, two people love each other more than they need each other. Because of this, the relationship itself becomes a safe haven to practice love. And love, ultimately, is a practice—a daily rehearsal of honesty, presence, communication, acceptance, forgiveness, and heartfelt patience.

Sadly, too often we forget the practicing part and we default instead to treating love like it's a guaranteed destination we can jump to whenever we have time. We want to arrive at that "perfect" loving feeling in a relationship without putting in the work. And when it doesn't work out that way, we assume the relationship itself is broken. But this is missing the whole point of a relationship—and the whole point of love.

Again, love is a practice. It's the daily commitment to embrace the unexpected and inconvenient qualities of a relationship, taking a deep breath, and asking yourself, "What part of love needs to be practiced here?" The answer will vary from one encounter

> **Love is a practice.**

to the next, in a continuous stream of tenderness, affection, and wisdom you could never have dreamed of or planned for.

Always Watch Your Response

When something stressful happens in a social situation, what is your default response? Some people jump right into action, but often immediate action can be harmful. Others get angry or sad. Still others start to feel sorry for themselves and victimized, wondering why other people can't behave better.

Responses like these are not healthy or helpful. In fact, whenever your response lacks a mindful level of acceptance, you're likely taking things too personally. And you're not alone. We all make this mistake sometimes. If someone does something we disagree with, we tend to interpret this as a personal attack.

- Our significant other doesn't show affection? They must not care about us as much as they should.
- Our children don't clean their rooms? They are purposely defying us.
- Our coworkers act inconsiderately at work? They must hate us.
- Someone hurts us? Everyone must be out to get us.

Some people even think life itself is personally against them. But the truth is, almost nothing in life is personal—things happen, or they don't, and it's rarely all about anyone specifically. People have emotional issues they're dealing with, and it makes them defiant, rude, and thoughtless sometimes. They are often doing the best they can, or they're not even aware of their issues. In any case, you can learn not to interpret their behaviors as personal attacks, and instead see them as nonpersonal encounters (like a dog barking in the distance, or a bumblebee buzzing by) that you can either respond to with a peaceful mind-set, or not respond to at all.

But what if a person's actions actually are directed at you for something you did? Perhaps you made a mistake that annoyed them and now they're deliberately reacting rudely toward you. A situation like this might seem personal, but is it really? Is the magnitude of their rude reaction all about you and the one thing you did to trigger them? No, probably not. Again, it's mostly just a statement about the other person's reactions, snap-judgments, anger issues, and expectations of the universe. You are a small piece of a much longer story.

But because we as human beings see everything through a lens of how it affects us—a lens that does a poor job of seeing the bigger picture—we tend to react to everyone else's actions as if they are a personal judgment about us. Thus, other people's anger makes us angry. Other people's lack of respect makes us feel unworthy. Other people's unhappiness makes us unhappy. And so it goes.

Realize this. Catch yourself. It's time to stop reacting . . . it's time to start watching your response.

The Toxic Behaviors That Tear Relationships Apart

What happens when the advice in this chapter falls by the wayside? Relationship toxicity ensues. And believe it or not, roughly 90 percent of the failing relationships we've witnessed and coached people through over the years suffered from one or more of the following six behaviors. (Note: We've found various books and works by psychologist Dr. John Gottman helpful in our evaluation, clarification, and classification of these particular toxic relationship behaviors.)

1. **Using complaints and disagreements as an opportunity to condemn each other.**

Complaints are okay. Disagreements are okay too. These are natural, honest reactions to a person's decisions or behavior. But when complaints and disagreements spiral out of control into global attacks on the person, and not on their decisions or behavior, trouble ensues. For example: "He didn't call me when he said he would, not because he was busy and forgot, but because he is a horrible, wretched, evil person." Remember, there's a big difference between who someone *is* and what he or she sometimes *does*.

> There's a big difference between who someone is and what he or she sometimes does.

2. **Using angry expressions as a substitute for honest communication.**

In whatever form, actions such as frequent name-calling, threats, eye rolling, belittling, mockery, and hostile teasing are poisonous to a relationship because they convey contempt. And it's virtually impossible to resolve a relationship problem when the other person is constantly receiving the message that you hate them.

Also, remember that if someone you love makes a mistake and you choose to forgive them, your actions must reinforce your words. In other words, let bygones be bygones. Don't use their past wrongdoings to justify your present righteousness. When you constantly use someone's past transgressions to make yourself seem "better" than them ("I'm better than you because, unlike you, I didn't do XYZ in the past"), it's a lose–lose situation.

Replace your negative thoughts with positive communication. Because the truth is, if you're throwing hateful gestures at a person instead of communicating with them, there's a good chance they don't even know why. Remind yourself that when communication between two people isn't open and honest, a lot of important things are never said.

3. **Denying responsibility for your role in the relationship.**

When you deny responsibility in relationship disputes, all you're really doing is blaming the other person. You're saying, in effect, "The problem here is never me, and it's always you." This denial of accountability just escalates every argument, because there's a complete breakdown in communication.

The key thing to understand is that you have a choice. Either you're choosing to be in a relationship with another person or you aren't. If you're choosing to be in, then you are responsible for it. Denying this means you're giving up all your power to the other person—you're their victim, regardless of circumstances (positive or negative), because you've given them 100 percent of the responsibility for the relationship.

So remember, even when the behavior driving a relationship dispute belongs to the other person, the only way to find common ground, or simply create more

healthy space for yourself, is to first accept that you are
50 percent responsible for the relationship at all times.
Once you do, you have the power to make progress one
way or the other.

4. **The silent treatment.**

   Tuning out, ignoring, disengaging, refusing to
acknowledge, and so on are all variations of the silent
treatment. They don't just remove the other person from
the argument you're having with them, they remove them
emotionally from the relationship. When you're ignoring
someone, you're really teaching them to live without you.
If that's what you want, be clear about it. And if not,
drop it!

5. **Using emotional blackmail.**

   Emotional blackmail happens when you apply an
emotional penalty against someone if they don't do exactly
what you want them to do. The key condition here is that
they change their behavior, against their will, as a result of
the emotional blackmail. In other words, absent the
emotional blackmail they would live differently, but they
fear the penalty—or punishment—and they give in. This is
an extremely unhealthy relationship behavior.

   The solution, again, relies heavily on better
communication. There should *not* be a penalty, just an
honest conversation. If two people care about each other
and want to maintain a healthy relationship, they
absolutely need to be "allowed" to openly communicate
all of their true feelings to each other, not just the
agreeable and positive ones. If this is not allowed or
supported by one or both people involved in the

relationship—if one or both people fear punishment for their honesty—lies and deceit will gradually replace love and trust, which ultimately leads to a complete emotional disconnection.

6. **Codependency and entitlement.**

When your actions and thoughts revolve around another person at the expense of your own individuality, that's codependency. When you believe another person inherently owes you something, that's entitlement. Both of these relationship traits are extremely harmful.

Remember that a healthy relationship never limits you, it doesn't restrict you, it doesn't try to change you, and it doesn't entitle you, or anyone, to anything.

People sometimes develop a sense of entitlement because they mistakenly believe they are owed something based solely on the social role they have chosen. For example, if someone has accepted the role of being a person's friend, girlfriend, boyfriend, wife, or husband, they feel entitled to certain "favors" from this person. If someone has accepted the role of being a parent, they feel entitled to respect from their children. If someone has accepted the role of being a customer, they feel entitled to having their unique needs served.

> A healthy relationship never limits you.

But, as it turns out, there are no guaranteed entitlements in life. And this is especially true of the love present in a healthy relationship.

Too often we associate love with limitations:

"If he loves me, he will change."

"If she loves me, she will do what I say."

"If they love me, they will know what I need."

But that's not real, healthy love. Not even close. That's the breeding ground for codependency and entitlement.

What we need instead is a healthy dose of self-sufficiency. As motivational speaker Jim Rohn once said, "The greatest gift you can give somebody is your own personal development. I used to say, 'If you will take care of me, I will take care of you.' Now I say, 'I will take care of me for you, if you will take care of you for me.'"

The Importance of Chemistry

Unfortunately, even if you're doing your best to practice all the qualities of a conscious, loving relationship, and avoid the aforementioned toxic behaviors, there's one key factor that can make it difficult or even impossible to ultimately build a healthy, nontoxic partnership: chemistry. When it comes to our important relationships, there are some people who bring energy into your life and some who suck it right out of you. That's the way chemistry works. Often we get so caught up in a single, powerful aspect of our attraction or connection to another person that we lose sight of the ways in which we're not quite suited for them and vice versa.

It's important to remember that it's possible for two people to be toxic to *each other* without necessarily being toxic as individuals. Each individual, as a unique and incredible human being, may be able to do amazing things and have great relationships with other people. But these two people might have certain characteristics and qualities that are like oil and water when they come together; there's just no mixing it.

We've seen this several times through our coaching. We've heard husbands and wives say, "I admire my significant other or my ex-significant other. She's a great person. But when we're together, it's not great." Chemistry is real, and it's crucial to recognize the role it plays in our relationships. At the very least, it's something to keep in mind if you find yourself desperately struggling to develop a new intimate relationship or friendship with someone.

What can help in any case, regardless of the uncontrollable elements of chemistry, is sincere honesty and better communication.

The Power of Communication

Recently, a busy attorney named Valentina (one of our past students) and her ten-year-old son, Marco, moved into their new home in New England. The winter season was already in full effect, and a massive snowstorm swept through the area the morning after they moved, closing all the schools.

Marco had a snow day, but Valentina still needed to visit her office for a couple of hours to finish up some important work for a new client. So despite the snowstorm, Valentina drove to work, leaving Marco in their nearly snowed-in home to work on his homework assignments.

Shortly after Valentina arrived at her office she received a text message from Marco that read: "Windows completely frozen. Will not open."

Valentina squinted at her phone in confusion, because she couldn't fathom why Marco wanted to open any of the windows. But she was busy and about to head into a meeting, so she didn't have time to sort out the details. She quickly texted Marco a simple fix she had learned as a young girl growing up in the mountains: "Warm up a cup of water in the microwave, pour it evenly over the edges, then lightly tap the edges with a mallet."

Valentina then hurried into her business meeting. When it was over, she saw that she had text messages from her son at home.

The first text from Marco read, "What? Are you sure that works?" Then, "Please hurry up! I have to turn in my essay soon!" Finally, "The laptop is dead!"

Confused by the messages, Valentina called Marco. He picked up, irritated and distraught.

"First . . . what's wrong with the laptop?" Valentina asked.

"I don't know," Marco replied. "I poured warm water over all of its edges and tapped them with a mallet, just like you told me to. But now it won't even turn on."

Valentina suddenly realized her ten-year-old son's initial text message was not about the windows of their new home. Rather, he had texted her about the Windows operating system that runs his laptop! Marco's computer was simply frozen, but now, thanks to a cup of warm water and the light tapping of a mallet, it was indeed dead!

When Valentina shared this story with us, we laughed along with her. It was a great reminder that in life, in business, and especially in our relationships, the biggest mistakes can arise from the smallest misunderstandings. Happily, we can avoid these misunderstandings with a simple approach: slow down, listen to others, and clarify what they mean. Yes, it will take a few more moments of your time. But it will also save you from painful headaches and heartache later on.

Mantras to Stop Misunderstandings

Truth be told, much of the unhappiness in the world is the result of bewilderment and things left miscommunicated. We know how misunderstandings can tear us apart. We know how healthier communication leads to healthier relationships. And yet we still often forget. We forget to make time for each other. We forget to be present. We forget to *really* listen. Day after day, we collectively misunderstand each other into hundreds of unnecessary headaches and heartbreaking mistakes.

And, like you, we're only human—we still miscommunicate and misunderstand people, especially when we're in a hurry. So we've implemented a simple strategy to support the practice of paying better attention to the people in our life. In a nutshell, we proactively remind ourselves of a few simple truths we already know but often forget. Anytime we catch ourselves avoiding a conversation we know we need to have with someone, we pause and read the following mantras. Afterward, it's easier to tune in to the person with our full presence.

1. The single greatest problem in communication is the illusion that it has taken place.
2. Too often we don't listen to understand—we listen to reply. Don't do this. Focus. Be curious. When we listen with genuine curiosity, we don't listen with the intent to reply—we listen for what's truly behind the words.
3. When you hear only what you want to hear, you're not really listening. Listen to what you don't want to hear too. That's how we grow stronger together.

4. You never know what someone has been through today. So don't be lazy and make empty judgments about them or their situation. Be kind. Be teachable. Be a good friend. Be a good neighbor. Be a good listener.

5. Sometimes all a person needs is an empathetic ear—they just need to know someone else hears them. Simply listening and offering a kind heart for their suffering can be incredibly healing.

6. Do not make assumptions unless you know the whole story. If in doubt, ask the person directly until you have clarity.

7. When you take the time to actually listen, with humility, to what people have to say, it's amazing what you can learn. Especially if the people who are doing the talking also happen to be the people you love.

If we had a dollar for every time we've heard about an unfortunate life situation directly caused by a combination of excessive busyness and poor communication, we would be able to send everyone we know an inscribed gold plaque of Valentina and Marco's story as a wake-up call. And although Valentina and Marco's story involves a mother-son relationship, think about how their miscommunication could easily bring toxicity into an intimate relationship or friendship. Sometimes the very reason there is no chemistry is simply that there is no communication.

Environment and the Far-Reaching Power of Those Around You

Let's shift gears for a moment and take a close, hard look at how the people around you affect you. Jim Rohn has said, "You are the average of the five people you spend the most time with." And nothing could be closer to the truth.

It's hard to deny the fact that who you are around on a regular basis drastically influences the person you will become. And it's not just your closest friends who can have this effect. Simply by being around others regularly, we begin to absorb their characteristics, behaviors, and intentions.

If you're trying to live a happier, more fulfilling life, you want to be around people who are interested in the positive growth you want too. People who hang around others who make more money typically make more money. People who hang around others who eat heathy tend to eat healthy too. Although this doesn't need to be true of everyone around you, you should try to choose environments populated by people who embody what you want to achieve.

For example, we attend a gym where lots of bodybuilders and physically fit fitness models work out. Walking into that gym, we immediately feel inspired. People of all ages, genders, and backgrounds are working hard, sweating, pumping. In this environment, you can't help but think, "Put a little more weight on that rack. I know I can do it!" There's no question that we are in better shape right now because we're working out in this gym. When we get there, it inspires us to push ourselves harder than we would without the visual inspiration. Does everyone in our life need to be heavily into fitness? No. But when we put ourselves in that setting, we're seeing people working harder than we are, and it pushes us to give it our best too.

No matter how much determination and willpower you have, if you keep yourself in an environment that works against your best intentions, you will eventually succumb to that environment. This is where so many of us take life-altering missteps. Rather than working in a supportive environment that pushes us forward, we expend all our energy trying to pull the baggage of an unhealthy environment along with us. And eventually, despite our best efforts, we run out of energy.

If this is your current situation, you'll need to set clear boundaries, dedicate yourself to the outcome you intend to achieve, and then reconfigure your environment to make that goal possible. Let's think about some other examples:

- If you want to lose weight, your best bet is to spend more time in healthy environments with people who eat healthy and exercise on a regular basis.
- If you want to become a paid, professional comedian— a goal one of our recent conference attendees recently achieved—surround yourself with professional comedians, do gigs together, share experiences, and reconfigure your living and working environment accordingly.
- If you want to overcome your struggles and live a happier life, spend more time communicating with people who share these same intentions.

The truth is that determination and willpower alone will only get you so far. We adapt to our surroundings. So if you want to intentionally guide your own growth and evolution, you need to decisively choose or create enriching environments where you'll be surrounded by people who influence you to achieve your desired outcomes.

The Delicate Art of Handling Difficult People

No matter how hard we try to surround ourselves with supportive people, difficult people will still find their way into our lives. Regardless of our age or social status, there will always be some individuals who want nothing more than to bully and belittle us. Sometimes they're colleagues at work, sometimes they're people in our neighborhoods, sometimes they're mean kids on the playground. And just as difficult people will always exist in the world, so too will our power to choose how we respond to them. Do we let them make their pain our own? Or do we choose to transform that pain into personal growth and strength? Do we let them win? Or do we choose to win?

It's hard to make wise choices in the heat of the moment. But when we choose to win and transform pain into personal growth and strength, we aren't just improving our own lives, we're improving the lives of the people we love and the people who look up to us.

Nonetheless, sometimes handling difficult people—and "winning"—is, well, difficult! We have worked with hundreds of students and clients over the past decade who were struggling through this very challenge. Here are five smart yet simple strategies that work wonders:

1. **Wish them well and move forward with your day.**

    Don't lower your standards, but do remember that removing your expectations of others is the best way to avoid being disappointed by them. Realize that there's no reason to expect others to treat you the way you treat them—not everyone has the same heart as you. Meditate on that. Let it sink in. Ultimately, the real test is being kind to unkind people. And yes, you can always stand tall and sincerely be kind to people you strongly disagree with.

Remind yourself that you never know what someone has been through in their life, or what they're going through today. Just do your best to be kind, generous, and respectful, no matter what. Truth be told, all the hardest, coldest people you meet were once as innocent as a baby. So when people are rude and difficult, be mindful—be your best. Give those around you the "break" that you hope the world will give you on your own bad day, and you will never, ever regret it.

2. Model the behavior you want to see.

When someone insists on foisting their hostility and drama on you, be an example of a pure existence. Ignore their outlandish antics and focus on compassion. Communicate and express yourself from a place of peace and love, with the best intentions. Use your voice for good, to inspire, encourage, educate, and spread the type of behavior you want to see in others.

This, of course, is much easier said than done. It takes long-term practice. Even with decades of practice behind us, we sometimes catch ourselves being rude to people who are rude to us—we behave badly because they behaved badly. And even if the situation is absolutely their fault, our behavior only escalates the situation. So we do our best to take a deep breath and set a good example of how to deal with anger and frustration. We try to be patient and compassionate with them—to demonstrate a positive way of handling difficult people. And doing so always helps us make progress, even if it's not instantaneous.

3. **Take positive control of negative conversations.**

It's okay to change the topic, talk about something positive, or steer conversations away from pity parties, drama, and self-absorbed sagas. Be willing to disagree with difficult people and deal with the consequences. Some people really don't recognize their own difficult tendencies or their inconsiderate behavior.

It can be okay to say, "I feel like you ignore me until you need something." You can also be honest if their overly negative attitude is what's driving you away: "I'm trying to focus on positive things. What's something good we can talk about?" It may work and it may not, but your honesty will help ensure that any communication that continues is built on mutually beneficial ground.

4. **Proactively establish healthy and reasonable boundaries.**

Practice becoming aware of your social feelings and needs. Note the times and circumstances when you're resentful of fulfilling someone else's needs. Gradually build boundaries by saying no to gratuitous requests that cause resentfulness in you. Of course, this will be hard at first because it may feel a bit selfish. But if you've ever flown on an airplane, you know that flight attendants instruct passengers to put on their own oxygen masks before tending to others, even their own children. Why? Because you can't help other people if you're incapacitated.

In the long run, establishing and enforcing healthy and reasonable boundaries with difficult people will be one of the most charitable things you can do for yourself and those you care about. These boundaries will foster and preserve the best of you, so you can share the best of yourself with the people who matter most, not just the difficult ones who bring you down.

5. **Be less difficult and more flexible yourself.**

It doesn't help to tame all the difficult people in your life if you're not ready to foster genuine relationships with kind people. On occasion, you may find that the difficulties between you and someone else evaporate when you start being less difficult yourself. Honestly, we're not trying to preach; this is something we're working on in our own lives—it's a lifelong practice.

Make that first call, offer a genuine compliment, schedule a fun outing with another person's preferences in mind, send that ridiculously funny text message for no real reason—there are tons of ways to nurture relationships with kind people who are worth the extra effort and sacrifice. And when good people and good intentions surround you, it's amazing how unnecessary pettiness, toxicity, and difficulty simply disappear from your conscious awareness.

This goes back to the point above on modeling the behavior you want to see. Just as light will dispel darkness, your light can be a shining example to everyone around you, including those who mean well but don't realize their difficult tendencies. And even though you'll likely need to limit your exposure to some people, don't underestimate the possibility that your example may influence them for the greater good, one way or the other, in the long run.

Our Rituals to Foster Healthy Relationships

Over the years, we've developed some rituals that help us stay mindful about these issues and foster the types of relationships that are healthy, loving, and long lasting. Let's use our relationship as an example:

As a married couple, we have our disagreements. But at the end of the day, we're here for each other. Regardless of any issue between us, we always kiss each other good night and say, "I love you." It doesn't matter if we're not seeing eye to eye at present. We love each other, in this moment and in all moments, and we support each other with positive language and gestures. That is a ritual that we practice every day, no matter what.

Another relationship ritual has to do with the idea that family time is nonnegotiable. We stop working at 4 p.m., then take time to eat dinner and relax with our son until 7 p.m. During those three hours, we stay present, and we let the day take us wherever it wants to go. We make sure to make time to sit down, be together, and discuss our day.

Sometimes we get caught up in passion projects and new ideas and lose focus on our family temporarily. And that's okay. It just means we have to be present enough to realize that we're losing sight of what means the most to us. Once we see that happening, we know we have to shift things around and prioritize our relationship with each other and our son—it's the awareness of what's most important that brings us back on track.

Finally, we always make sure any disagreement isn't an excuse to be mean to each other. When we're having an argument, we consciously choose words that add value to the conversation and help achieve a resolution. Sometimes you need to give constructive criticism. But whatever you say—whether it's easy to hear or not—needs to be kind, and it needs to add *real* value.

These are just a few small rituals that are currently helping us foster a strong relationship with each other. These practices may look different in other relationships, and they don't apply only to romantic relationships. We also have rituals to help foster the other important relationships in our lives. For instance, we make sure to meet a few of our closest friends once a month and have lunch. It's very important to us to make sure we're appreciating the important people in our lives and enjoying their company.

The bottom line is this: communicating with the people who matter—people who add value to your life—is an essential thing.

> Stay connected to the people who lift you up.

It's easy to be busy with everything else. The question is: what, and who, is truly important to you? If a person is important, schedule them in. If it's not possible to get together, make a phone call. Send an email. It can be that small. Stay connected to the people who lift you up. Just making sure they know you want to check up on them and tell them you love and miss them can make a big difference.

Closing Exercise
Spend fifteen minutes of quality time every day with someone you love, with no major agenda and no technology.

Put down the smartphone, close the laptop, and enjoy each other's company, face-to-face, the old-fashioned way. There are few joys in life that equal a good conversation, a genuine laugh, a long walk, a friendly dance, or a big hug shared by two people who care about each other. Sometimes the most ordinary things can be made extraordinary just by doing them with the right people. So choose to be around these people and make the most of your time together. Don't wait to make big plans. Make your time together the plan. Communicate openly on a regular basis. Get together in the flesh as often as possible. Not because it's convenient to do so, but because you know the other person is worth the extra effort.

CHAPTER 9

Happiness: Nurture an Inner and Outer Environment That Fulfills You

Happiness isn't out there, waiting to be found—it's in you, waiting to be embraced.

Our phone rang just before midnight. I grabbed it off the nightstand, and we both squinted at its bright screen. "Claire," it read. Claire is a close friend who tragically lost her husband to cancer last year. It was rare for her to call at such a late hour, so it had to be important.

We answered the phone and she burst into tears when we asked her what was wrong. She said she needed help. She'd just lost her job, she felt exhausted yet couldn't sleep, and she didn't know how to move forward. We admitted to her that we sometimes didn't know either, but we did know that a job was just a job, and that Angel's job loss had been a blessing in disguise.

Sighing through her tears, she explained how she felt like she was barely maintaining her balance and that it felt as if she might fall at any moment. These feelings kept her in a vicious loop: one good day followed by multiple bad days. The only thing that seemed to help her was a saying her grandmother taught her as a child: do your best with what's in front of you and leave the rest to the powers above you.

We smiled. It reminded Marc of a short story his grandmother told him—one that was also applicable to Claire's circumstances. So we told her the story:

> Once upon a time, in a small village, the village fisherman accidentally dropped his favorite fishing pole into the river and was unable to retrieve it. When his neighbors heard of his loss, they came over and said, "That's just bad luck!" The fisherman replied, "Perhaps."
>
> The following day, the fisherman hiked a mile down the bank of the river to see if he could find his fishing pole. He came upon a small alcove in the riverbank that was loaded to the brim with salmon. He used his backup fishing pole to catch nearly one hundred salmon, loaded them into his wagon, and brought them back to the village. Everyone was ecstatic to receive the fresh salmon. When his neighbors caught word of his success, they came over and said, "Wow! What great luck you have!" The fisherman replied, "Perhaps."
>
> Two days later, the fisherman began hiking back toward the alcove so he could catch more salmon. But he tripped on a tree stump and severely sprained his ankle. He slowly and painfully hopped back to the village to nurse his health. When his neighbors caught word of his injury, they told him, "That's just bad luck!" The fisherman replied, "Perhaps."
>
> Four days went by, and although the fisherman's ankle was slowly healing, he could not yet walk, and the village was

completely out of fish to eat. Three other villagers volunteered to go to the river to fish while the fisherman recovered. That evening, when the three men did not return, the village sent a search party out for them, only to discover that the men had been attacked and killed by a pack of wolves. When the fisherman's neighbors caught word of this, they said, "You're so lucky you weren't out there fishing. What great luck you have!" The fisherman replied, "Perhaps."

"A few days later . . . well, you can guess how the story continues," Marc said, and Claire chuckled softly, thanking him for sharing the story. Because the moral of the story was immediately clear to her. Life is unpredictable. No matter how good or bad things seem right now, we can never be certain what will happen next.

The unpredictability of life is an ultimate truth we need to accept. But that doesn't mean we are powerless. It doesn't mean we don't have many, many options to create meaning and purpose, to find joy amid all the unpredictability. No matter the uncertainty of life, you are capable of cultivating happiness and getting yourself closer to the life you want to lead.

Throughout the book, we've discussed a lot of strategies to help you along that path. We've covered the power of daily rituals and mindfulness practices that can help you shift your mindset, how to change your situation for the better, and how to find that elusive motivation. All of these ideas and frameworks are aimed at helping you do what the title of this book says: getting you back to happy.

In this chapter, we'd like to expand on some key ideas and proven strategies that we know will help you do just that.

Happiness Must Be Cultivated from Within

So often, people will tell you to go out and find happiness, as though it's such a simple commodity that you could stroll down to your local grocery store and pluck it off a shelf. Happiness, however, is not found somewhere else; it's grown and developed inside of you. No one is going to come over and save you and give you happiness. Your happiness is up to you, and you alone.

There's an interesting little wrinkle when it comes to the individuality of happiness, though. Through all of the coaching we've done over the years, we've seen how different people seem to have a different *baseline* of happiness, so to speak. Some people are just generally happier than others. But even for those people whose baseline may be less happy, they still have great potential to cultivate happiness. It all comes down to focus and mindset.

We've seen the power of focus and mindset, of intentionally cultivating happiness, in action. Through our coaching with our clients and students, and even at our live events, it's unbelievable how often immense personal changes can be traced back to a shift in mental attitude. We've seen how simple mindset tactics like self-inquiry, for example, are liberating for people who are stressed out or unhappy about their present circumstances. After all, you can't always change your circumstances, but you can always change your attitude about your circumstances. The problem, then, isn't the problem. The problem is the way you're thinking about it.

When your mindset is in order, you can nurture an inner and outer environment in which you can cultivate your own happiness. It can be as simple as being aware of what's troubling your worried mind and then asking yourself the questions discussed in the "Practicing Self-Inquiry Through Journaling" section of chapter 4:

- Can I be absolutely certain that this troubling thought is true?
- How do I feel and behave when I think this thought?
- How might I feel, and what else might I see, if I erased this troubling thought from my mind right now?
- What's one other reasonable possibility that might also be true?
- What's the complete opposite of this troubling thought, and is there any truth in this opposing thought?

Simple questions like these are incredibly powerful; when used consciously and regularly, they can free our minds from all kinds of self-limiting thoughts and beliefs. You may also want to reread the related closing exercise of chapter 3.

Ease Your Craving to Control the Uncontrollable

As we've discussed throughout this book, letting go of control and being okay with it is one of the greatest struggles many of us deal with on a daily basis, ourselves included. Because letting go of control goes directly against our way of living—we are go-getters, doers, architects of our destiny. We build things and make things happen on our own terms; we don't wait for anything to happen on someone else's terms! At least that's what we often learn growing up from teachers, sports coaches, movies, pop songs, magazine articles, and so forth. Allowing things to happen is not exactly in our DNA. Many of us have never been ones to sit back and passively release control.

Over the years, however, our perspective has shifted. We've learned the hard way that a great deal of the control we believe we have over our lives is an illusion. We've met countless individuals whose lives have been turned upside down by illness, natural disasters, bankruptcy, and other tragic, unexpected circumstances.

It happens every day: we discover we don't really have control over situations we thought we did. So what can we do? The only choice we have: let go and be mindful.

In the game of life, we all receive a unique set of unexpected limitations and variables. The question is: how will you respond to the hand you've been dealt? You can either focus on what you are lacking or empower yourself to play the game sensibly and resourcefully, making the very best of every outcome as it arises, even when it's heartbreaking and hard to accept.

We've said it previously, and we'll say it again: the mind is our biggest battleground. It's the place where the strongest conflict resides. It's where half of the things we thought were going to happen never did happen. It's where our expectations always get the best of us. It's where we fall victim to our cravings to control the uncontrollable. And if we allow these thoughts and cravings to dwell in our minds, they will succeed in robbing us of peace, joy, and ultimately our lives. We will think ourselves into deep heartache and even depression.

> **The mind is our biggest battleground.**

Truthfully, there's so much about life that we can't control, it makes no sense to waste our energy on these things and then blatantly neglect everything we *can* control.

We can choose how we spend our time right now. We can

choose gratitude and grace. We can choose whom we socialize with—whom we share this day of our lives with. We can choose to love and appreciate the people in our lives for exactly who they are. We can choose to love and appreciate ourselves too. We can choose how we're going to respond to life's surprises and disappointments when they arise, and whether we will see them as problems or opportunities for personal growth. And, perhaps most important, we can choose to adjust our attitudes and let go of all our worries about everything we can't control, which in turn frees us up to take the next best step forward in our lives.

Stop Your Participation in Needless Drama

The previous discussion on letting go of control directly leads to this one: whenever we demand control over the uncontrollable, or stubbornly resist the present reality of our lives, needless drama ensues.

Drama is simply the consequence of how our mind interprets and conflicts with outer incidents. Thus, the drama you are going through at any given moment is not fueled by the words or deeds of others, or any external sources at all; it is fueled primarily by your mind, which gives the drama importance.

And yes, we all do this to ourselves sometimes. But why? Why do we get so easily stressed out and sucked into drama? It's because the world isn't the predictable, orderly, blissful place we'd like it to be. We want things to be easy, comfortable, and well ordered 24/7. Unfortunately, sometimes work is hectic, relationships are challenging, people demand our time, we aren't as prepared as we'd like to be, our family frustrates us, and there's just too much to do and learn and process in our minds. So our inner conflict begins to boil over.

But again, the problem isn't the world, or other people's thoughts and behavior—these aspects of life will always be a slightly unpredictable mess. The problem is that we're holding on too tightly to ideals that don't match reality. We have subconsciously set up expectations in our minds of what we want other people to be, what we want ourselves to be, and what our work and relationships and life "should" be like. Our attachment to our ideals stirs anxiety in our minds and stress in our lives.

In other words, our resistance to accept things as they are fuels our drama. And we don't want to be a part of this drama—at least that's what we tell ourselves—so we blame others for it, which in turn creates even more drama.

But as we've discussed throughout this book, we can let go of drama and find peace with reality. And although there are many ways of doing so, I'm going to suggest a simple practice to start with for whenever you feel stress, resistance, frustration, worry, and all the other draining mindsets that fuel drama in your life:

Focus carefully on what you're feeling. Don't numb it with distractions, but instead bring it further into your awareness.

- Turn to it and welcome it. Smile and give what you feel is your full, thoughtful attention.
- Notice the feeling in your body. Where is the feeling situated, and what unique qualities does it have?
- Notice the tension in your body, and also in your mind, that arises from this feeling.
- Try relaxing the tense parts of your body. Then relax the tense parts of your mind. Do so by focusing on your breath: close your eyes, breathe in and feel it, breathe out and feel it, again and again, until you feel more relaxed.

Then, in this more relaxed state, find some quiet space within yourself. And in this space:

- Allow yourself to rediscover the fundamental goodness within you that's present in every moment.
- Allow yourself to rediscover the fundamental goodness of this very moment, which is always available to you whenever you're willing to focus on it.
- Finally, take time to just sit with the inner peace these two simple rediscoveries bring.

This is the practice of letting go of drama and simply accepting this moment as it is, and yourself as you are. You can do this anytime, wherever you are. You can practice focusing on the goodness in others as well—seeing the goodness in your challenges and relationships and work, and so forth. You can build a healthy daily ritual of stopping the needless drama in your life, and rediscovering the peace and joy and love that are always just a few thoughts away.

See Your Biggest Problems as Opportunities

We hope you've begun to appreciate the fact that although the world is not out to get you, it will absolutely continue to throw you curveballs—sometimes big ones. But it's in those unforeseen "disasters," those ultrachallenging moments, that we can often find the greatest opportunity for growth and cultivating happiness by recalibrating our mind-set.

As an example, let's say a person is going through a divorce and they find themselves thinking: "I won't be able to get past this.

There's no way I can get beyond the pain of this divorce." If they're thinking this way, it's easy to see how discouraged they must feel. They're not going to take any steps forward because they don't see the point in doing so. But taking the time to ask themselves, "Is that really true? Can I be *absolutely* certain that thought is true?" can offer insight into how they're framing their situation, and whether that frame is helpful or even valid. When we encourage our clients and students to question their subconscious thoughts in this way, they usually come to realize that the *way* they're thinking about the situation is adding more anxiety and grief than necessary, and preventing them from finding a way through.

So instead of thinking, "This divorce is the worst thing that ever happened to me," they might practice thinking, "This divorce is an opportunity." It doesn't mean that the situation didn't happen, or that it isn't terrible and heartbreaking, or difficult financially or emotionally. It means there are other potentially positive aspects to focus on in spite of this heartbreaking situation, and by doing so, we can allow glimmers of opportunity for growth and happiness to shine through. In this way, we don't have to wait for positive moments to come to us once our sadness starts to finally, inevitably fade, but we can instead start cultivating positive moments in the bedrock of even our most painful experiences.

Move Your Body into Happiness

In all this talk of mindset, it's important to remember that your body is also incredibly powerful when it comes to cultivating happiness and developing a positive frame for your life. Happiness comes from within you, from realizing that you have control over the way you think about what's going on—and you'll be better equipped to achieve this potential for happiness when your body and mind are working together.

Remember what we discussed in the closing exercise of chapter 6: in many ways, the mind drives the body, but the body drives the mind too. When it comes to cultivating happiness for ourselves, the way we use our bodies unquestionably affects everything. Various psychological studies have proven that our bodies can directly affect our mental state of being. So while it's true that we change from the inside out, we also change from the outside in.

Moving your body can be directly beneficial to your state of mind and happiness, whether it's by making you stronger or giving you a rush of endorphins after a long run. But more than just that, moving your body is also a great way to change your situation and your environment. If you're feeling negative in your current position or routine, simply breaking out of that routine with a change to your physical environment or physical activity can do wonders for your mind's health. Plus, moving your body in different ways and into different places helps you experience novelty—new sights, sounds, and environments that can broaden your horizon and shift your perspective for the better.

Gradually Eliminate the Excess

As they say, "Nobody can go back and start a new beginning, but anyone can start today and make a new ending." But before you can begin this process of transformation, you have to stop doing the things that have been holding you back.

Remember, when you stop chasing after the wrong things, you give the right things a chance to catch up with you. It's all about becoming conscious of how you are allocating your limited time and energy, so you can put yourself in a position to build the future you want. Think about your own life and the lives of those close to you. Most of us have a tendency to do as much as we possibly can—cramming every waking minute with events, extravagances, tasks, and obligations. And we just keep running in place.

We think doing more will get us more satisfaction, success, etc., when often the exact opposite is true. In his acclaimed productivity book *Getting Things Done,* David Allen explains that some things in life and business are important in the long run, while most things are *only* pressing in the moment. Too many people spend all the days of their lives working on pressing, unimportant activities. Very few of us have focused our time and energy in a way that mindfully prioritizes truly important and meaningful objectives over everything else that pops up.

When it comes to managing our time and energy, less is indeed more! Thus, the smartest and most effective way to move forward in life is not doing more, but instead doing less by eliminating the excess that gets in your way.

- If you want to lose weight, you'll only make sustainable progress by first reducing your unhealthy daily rituals before you rush to start a bunch of new healthy ones. So, for example, before you start forcing yourself to hit the gym every morning at 5 a.m., first eliminate the excess sugar and saturated fat from your diet. Slapping a healthy workout on top of an unhealthy diet is like building a house on top of quicksand—it doesn't work out in the long run.
- If you want to become more financially stable, don't focus on increasing your income until you've addressed

your wasteful spending habits. Break yourself out of the cycle of needing more, and become content with what you have. Until you do so, it doesn't really matter how much you earn. You'll always spend every cent you have on things you don't need.

Organize yourself. Focus on what matters. And get rid of everything else. Do less, and make the less you do count for even more.

Look for Discomfort, Not Confidence

Taking the first step toward change—toward happiness—can seem scary, but in most cases, all you have to do is start. Often we shy away from taking that first step because we think we need more confidence. But we misinterpret how confidence works. We think confidence is something we have to possess before we can perform at our best. So we make a subconscious decision to wait until we feel more confident before taking the next step. But waiting around isn't a confidence-building activity, so we never feel more confident, and we never take action. Let this be your wake-up call.

Confidence is not a prerequisite to present and future performance; confidence is a direct result of past performance. If you begin a new project today and experience early glimmers of success, you're likely to have improved confidence tomorrow with the next phase of the project. Conversely, if the project gets off to a bumpy start, and your efforts today fall short, that prior performance will likely lower your confidence tomorrow (until your confidence level inevitably cycles again). But the real kicker is the fact that your confidence (the way you feel) going into tomorrow is directly dependent on your taking positive action today and learning from it. And this means two things:

- You can leverage your present actions to improve your future confidence.
- Forcing yourself to take the next step is the first step to feeling more confident (and generally happier too).

So whenever you catch yourself waiting around for more confidence to magically arrive before you start working on the task in front of you, remind yourself of how confidence works, then force yourself to start before you feel ready. The confidence will come *after you start*—after you get comfortable with the discomfort of starting before you feel ready.

We've discovered this in our own lives, over and over again. Getting comfortable with discomfort—and gradually building up our mental strength in the process—has easily been the biggest key to our long-term happiness and success. If you can learn to get comfortable with discomfort, your life will be filled with fewer limits and a lot more opportunities.

Start Small, and Notice Your Progress (the Journal Trick)

When we look back on this book, we're amazed that all of these strategies are tools we implement every day. A decade before, we would have thought writing this book was an impossibility. Part of what got us past that was embracing the power of starting small. Although it sounds obvious, we've learned through often difficult experiences that you don't ever get from point A to point B as fast as you'd like.

Taking small steps toward our goals took us from being very discouraged about a lot of things in our lives to being very hopeful about them. This doesn't mean we don't suffer anymore. Of course we do, but our mind-set is completely different now. We see possibility. We appreciate what we've got. We realize our immense potential.

Pick something you want to change, and work on it so it becomes a daily habit—make it a ritual. Just get started, and take it one step at a time. Things almost certainly won't change overnight, and the aching feeling of wanting a better day, to feel more lightness and joy, will still be there. But day by day, stick with your small rituals, your little steps. Then, all of a sudden, one day you'll wake up and say, "Wow. I feel more like myself. I feel happier." You likely won't be able to pinpoint that day ahead of time, but it'll come up on you gradually, then hit you, just like that.

In chapter 1, we talked about using a journal as a powerful tool for self-inquiry and self-reflection. We discussed how helpful this practice can be to keep yourself focused on staying present and being grateful for what you have while you're waiting for that day when things come together. Angel uses a journal to note little things in our daily lives that she finds successful, funny, challenging, or noteworthy in some way. By doing this, she has a catalog of items and anecdotes that she can look back on to reflect and see the progress she's made. Having that list helps her see how much she's grown, gives her perspective on her current struggles, and helps her appreciate how far she's come.

A Few More Things Happy People Do

There are a few more core practices that have been crucial for us in our quest to cultivate happiness in our lives, and although we've mentioned most of them in various parts of this book already, we'd be remiss if we didn't quickly summarize them here to close out our discussion on cultivating happiness.

1. **Give to others whenever you are able.** While giving is considered an unselfish act (and it is), giving can also be more beneficial for the giver than for the receiver. In many cases, providing social support is actually more beneficial to our happiness than receiving it. Happy people know this, which is precisely why they are always looking for ways to help others, while unhappy people stand around asking, "What's in it for me?"

2. **Say *no* when you need to.** Saying yes to everything puts you on the fast track to being miserable. Feeling like you're just doing busywork is often the result of saying yes to people too much. We all have obligations, but you can only find a comfortable pace by properly managing your commitments. So stop saying yes when you want to say no. You can't always be agreeable; that's how people take advantage of you. Sometimes you have to set clear boundaries.

3. **Practice gratitude.** Gratitude is arguably the king of happiness. What's the research say? It can't be any more clear than Sonja Lyubomirsky's insight in *The How of Happiness:* "The more a person is inclined to gratitude,

the less likely he or she is to be depressed, anxious, lonely, envious, or neurotic." Bottom line: consider every day how very fortunate you are. The more you count your blessings, the more blessings there will be to count, and the happier you will be.

4. **Cultivate optimism.** The happiest people live not with a certain set of circumstances, but with a certain set of attitudes. They have the ability to manufacture their own optimism. No matter the situation, the successful human is the one who will always find a way to put an optimistic spin on it. They know failure only as an opportunity to grow and learn a new lesson from life. People who think optimistically see the world as a place packed with endless opportunities, especially in trying times.

5. **Don't attach yourself to every success and failure.** Happy, successful people are often successful in the long run for one simple reason: they think about success and failure differently. They don't take everything that goes wrong personally, and they don't take credit when everything goes right. Follow in their footsteps. Be a humble, lifelong learner. Don't let your successes get to your head, and don't let your failures get to your heart.

6. **See rejection as protection from what's not meant to be.** Rejection doesn't mean you aren't good enough; it means the other person failed to notice what you have to offer. It means you have more time to improve your endeavors— to build upon your ideas, to perfect your craft, and to indulge deeper in the work that moves you. Happy people know this, and they don't take rejection personally. The guy who didn't call back, the potential

job that didn't pan out, or the business loan rejection letter are all universal signs that it wasn't the best fit. Trust that something better suited for you is on its way.

7. **Dedicate time to meaningful pursuits.** When *The Guardian* recently asked a hospice nurse about "the top five regrets of the dying," one of the most common regrets was that people regretted not being true to their dreams. When people realize that their life is almost over and look back clearly on it, it's easy to see how many dreams have gone unfulfilled. Most people do not honor even half of their dreams and end up dying knowing that their unfulfilled dreams were due to the choices they made or didn't make. Good health brings a freedom very few realize, until they no longer have it. As they say, there are seven days in the week, and "someday" isn't one of them.

8. **Commit fully to your top priorities.** If you're interested in something, you will do what is convenient. If you're committed to something, you will do whatever it takes. Period. And ultimately, it's commitment that creates outcomes worth smiling about.

9. **Take care of your physical health.** There's no getting around it: no matter how much you think you dislike exercise, it will make you feel better if you stick with it. If you don't have your physical energy, then your mental energy (your focus), your emotional energy (your feelings), and your spiritual energy (your purpose) will all be negatively affected. In fact, did you know that recent studies conducted on people who were battling depression showed that consistent exercise raises happiness levels just as much as most antidepressants? Even better, six months

later, the people who participated in exercise were less likely to relapse, because they had a higher sense of self-accomplishment and self-worth.

10. **Spend money on experiences rather than on needless stuff.** Happy people are often mindful of spending money on physical items, opting instead to spend much of their extra money on experiences. "Experiential purchases" tend to make us happier for two key reasons: 1) Great experiences improve over time when we reminisce about them, and 2) experiences are often social events that get us out of our house and interacting with people we care about.

11. **Savor life's little joys.** Happiness is a how, not a what—it's a mindset, not a destination. Happiness is enjoying all the small things, while chasing after the big ones. Deep happiness cannot exist without slowing down to savor the joy. It's easy in a world of wild stimuli and omnipresent movement to forget to embrace life's little enjoyable experiences. When we neglect to appreciate, we rob the moment of its magic. The simple things in life can be the most rewarding if we remember to fully experience them.

12. **Live a life you actually want to live.** One of the most common complaints we hear from coaching clients and course students is: "I wish I were brave enough to live a life I want to live, not the life everyone else expects me to live." Don't do this to yourself. What other people think—especially those you don't even know—doesn't matter. Your hopes, your dreams, your goals—they all matter! Make choices that feel right. Surround yourself

with people who support and care not for the "you" they want you to be, but for the real you. Make true friends and stay in touch with them. Say things you really want to say to the people who need to hear them. Express your feelings. Remember to be mindful, be present, enjoy what's right in front of you. And most of all, realize that happiness, or at least peace of mind, in most situations is a choice.

As Elbert Hubbard once said, "Happiness is a habit—cultivate it." And remember, you don't need any more confidence; you just need a willingness to start and to encounter a little discomfort along the way.

Closing Exercise

This simple exercise is the one we've found most consistently helpful in our lives over the years. Every evening before you go to bed, write down three things that went well during the day and their causes. Simply provide a short, causal explanation for each good thing. (For example, "I made it home safely from work today.")

That's it. We spend tens of thousands of dollars on expensive electronics, big homes, fancy cars, and lavish vacations hoping for a boost of happiness. This is a free alternative, and it works.

Research backs up its effectiveness. We tried it ourselves more than a decade ago—we set a goal of doing it for just one week, and we're still doing it today. So we can assure you, it's effective. If you begin this simple ritual today, you might look back on today as the day your whole life changed.

Afterword
(and Three Tiny Things to Do *Now*)

Let's bring this book full circle and leave off where we began.

You will never feel perfectly ready, and the moment will never be perfectly convenient—to start, to put in the effort, to learn as you go, to gradually get the hard things done. If it were easier and more convenient, everyone would be blissfully happy and incredibly successful. There would be no inner emotional conflicts. No pain. No unrealized dreams.

You absolutely have to do the hard things to be happy in life.

Too many amazing people are still waiting around for someone or something outside themselves to pick them up and carry them forward.

We know because we used to be those people.

But we changed.

And so can *you*.

If you want something from life—if you want to get back to

happy—you have to want it more than anything else. You have to start doing things today, and every day hereafter, that directly support the outcome you desire—the happiness you deserve. It may not be easy, but it is just that simple, and it is within your reach.

And for those who feel somewhat overwhelmed by everything we've covered together in this book, and all the positive work there is to do going forward, we will send you off with a final open letter.

An Open Letter to Those Who Are Overwhelmed (and Not Sure What to Do Next)

Just like the ones we shared back in chapters 4 and 7, this open letter was inspired by a short email we received recently from one of our newest course students:

> Dear Marc and Angel,
>
> I'm stuck in a rut. I have dozens of good ideas that I can easily execute, but every time I rev up to take action, I get overwhelmed and scared. I start second-guessing my choices and myself. Or I start worrying about and obsessing over all the possibilities for both success and failure, until everything comes to a halt and I'm utterly exhausted. There's so much I want to achieve, and I know I'm capable if I could just get beyond this. What do you recommend?
>
> Sincerely,
>
> An Overwhelmed Student

Our reply (an open reply to all who feel overwhelmed with taking the next step):

Dear Overwhelmed Student,

It's time for a quick story about life:

Once upon a time there was a woman who had been lost in the desert for three days without water. Just as she was about to collapse, she saw what appeared to be a lake just a few hundred yards in front of her. "Could it be? Or is it just a mirage?" she wondered.

With the last bit of strength she could muster, she staggered toward the lake and quickly learned that her prayers had been answered: it was no mirage—it was indeed a large, spring-fed lake full of fresh water—more fresh water than she could ever drink in her lifetime. Yet while she was literally dying of thirst, she couldn't bring herself to drink the water. She simply stood by the water's edge and stared down at it.

There was a passerby riding on a camel from a nearby desert town who was watching the woman's bizarre behavior. He got off his camel, walked up to the thirsty woman, and asked, "Why don't you have a drink, ma'am?"

She looked up at the man with an exhausted, distraught expression and tears welling up in her eyes. "I am dying of thirst," she said. "But there is way too much water here in this lake to drink. No matter what I do, I can't possibly finish it all."

The passerby smiled, bent down, scooped some water up with his hands, lifted it to the woman's mouth, and said, "Ma'am, your opportunity right now, and as you move forward throughout the rest of your life, is to understand that you don't have to drink the whole lake to quench your thirst. You can simply take one sip. Just one small sip . . . and then another if you choose. Focus only on the mouthful in front of you, and all your anxiety, fear, and distress about the rest will gradually fade."

Challenge yourself today to focus solely on the sip (task, step, ritual, etc.) you're actually taking.

Honestly, that's all life is—small, positive actions that you take moment by moment, and then one day when you look back it all adds up to something worthwhile—something that's often far better than and different from what you had imagined when you started.

Sincerely,

Marc and Angel

Three Tiny Things Worth Doing Now

We hope this book continues to be a trusted companion on your journey. Now that you've reached this point, we suggest you do three little things:

1. **Pick one closing exercise from the book and get started.** You can't do everything all at once. By trying to do too much you end up getting nothing done at all. So start with one of the rituals found at the end of each chapter in this book—the one you feel you're struggling the most with right now and that might have the most impact for you. Then commit to doing it for sixty days before starting on the next. Why sixty days? Because that is generally the amount of time it takes to build a ritual into your life. In fact, scientific studies have shown this to be the case.

   That's our challenge to you. Take one of the rituals, and for the next sixty days make it a part of your life. It doesn't have to be for much time each day—even just five or ten minutes. So take the calendar out, mark those sixty days, and put an X through every single day that you do the ritual. When you get to the end of that sixty days, pick up the next ritual, or increase the amount of time that you're doing the first one.

Anytime somebody tells us they're not achieving something, or reads a book and says, "That's great knowledge," but hasn't taken any action, they're not going to see the results they're looking for. For instance, if someone were to tell us, "It's impossible for me to get in shape," we'd ask, "Have you committed to your workout routine as a ritual for the past sixty days?" If the answer was, "No, I haven't," then we'd say, "Come back and talk to us when you've gone sixty days without missing a day." That's the simple difference between success and failure when it comes to achieving the outcomes you want in your life.

You can start small, but you need to begin, and you need to make it a daily ritual. So pick one and start today.

2. **Sign up for the *Marc & Angel Hack Life* email list.** The best lessons we learn in life are the ones we learn over and over again. We need positive reminders in order to take a positive step forward every day. That's what our email list is all about, picking right up where this book leaves off.

In our emails, you'll find a lot of ideas and strategies—powerful emotional, mental, and sometimes even physical tools—for happier living, the very ones we use in our lives and in our coaching to help people. Many of our readers respond to these emails time and again, saying, "I felt as though you were talking directly to me." In today's world, one filled with so much negativity and little talk of personal growth, you need an outlet that will give you a quick kick of inspiration, one that will help you feel as though somebody is talking and listening to you.

We're constantly revisiting a lot of our own material, taking older articles and updating and improving them based on our recent coaching client stories, and every week we write two original articles that go out to our subscribers. So if you want to keep your mind-set right, to continue to put your best foot forward, and to be reminded of the strategies you've learned in this book, sign up at: www.marcandangel.com/subscribe.

3. **Join the Marc & Angel Facebook Page.** This page is for readers of *Getting Back to Happy* and our blog. The Facebook page is where you'll find daily inspirations and can connect with others who have read this book and are ready to dig even deeper to create the lives they want to live. It's a perfect place for like-minded seekers of a happier life to share their stories, struggles, victories, and more. Find it at: www.facebook.com /marcandangelhacklife.

If You Want to Continue
Your Journey with Us

The Getting Back to Happy course is an online, self-paced course designed to help you take what you've learned in this book to the next level, with included one-on-one (and two-on-one) coaching directly from us.

Getting Back to Happy is the go-to course for anyone serious about taking action to reclaim their happiness and realize their potential. It will help you wake up every day and live with a fuller sense of purpose, even if you've tried everything else. If you've been wanting a way to work with us, this is it. It's the result of more than a decade of study and one-on-one coaching with hundreds of people just like you from all over the world. It's a proven system that works time and again to bust people out of their ruts and get them back on track to living a life they are excited about. From proven ways to foster stronger relationships to actions engineered to help you let go of painful emotions, the learning modules in this course will inspire and equip you to become your best self.

When you enroll in Getting Back to Happy, you'll receive access to a massive collection of helpful resources. From inspiring stories to actionable strategies to lots of live-engagement opportunities (phone calls and video calls) with us, Getting Back to Happy provides more than just great content: it fosters an uplifting community. Everyone who enrolls in Getting Back to Happy will get lifetime access to a supportive community and a self-paced online course that's packed with sixty HD video trainings, including hundreds of scientifically proven methods for getting back on track, and members-only discussion forums where you can discuss each lesson with both of us and other course members.

Learn more about Getting Back to Happy and enroll at: www .marcandangel.com/getting-back-to-happy.

The Think Better, Live Better live conference is the go-to event for you if you're serious about taking action to reclaim your happiness and realize your true potential. Think Better, Live Better is designed to help you wake up every day and live life with a full sense of purpose, even if you've tried everything else. If you want to attend a life-changing conference filled with world-class personal development experts who care, this is it!

Think Better, Live Better is packed full of practical strategies and unforgettably inspiring lessons for living a more positive and productive life. But this is more than just an event. It's an immersive experience that will give you proven tools to identify and transform the negative, self-limiting beliefs and behaviors that keep you stuck. From proven ways to foster healthier relationships, to actions engineered to help you let go of painful experiences and emotions, to rituals guaranteed to increase your productivity, the actionable talks and workshops at this event—delivered by some of the brightest minds in personal growth—will inspire and equip you to become your most effective self.

This event is your gateway to the life you've planned on living. You won't leave Think Better, Live Better with a notebook full of ideas and nothing checked off your to-do list. Instead, you'll set into motion a realistic plan you can keep improving on for years to come. We will guide you step-by-step through mental strength exercises, and help you refocus your mind on the powerful truths that will have the fastest and most effective impact on your personal and professional desires and goals.

Learn more and register for the next event at: thinklivebetter.com

Acknowledgments

Anaïs Nin profoundly said, "Each friend represents a world in us, a world possibly not born until they arrive, and it is only by this meeting that a new world is born." This book was undoubtedly conceived and born through the direct and indirect support we have received over the years from our "friends."

Some of our friends are family, some we've known since we were kids, and others are newer friendships that continue to grow stronger by the day. Although they are all very different, every one of them is extraordinary. And we are grateful for them.

To our parents, Drew, Deborah, Farrell, and Mary, thank you for being our greatest teachers. Thank you for walking the talk every step of the way. Thank you for showing us that being a parent is a daily attitude, not a biological relation. And most of all, thank you for teaching us how to think, not what to think. Because of you, we are.

To our son, Mac, thank you for lighting up our world with love. Your arrival into our lives changed everything in the most unimaginable, educational, and amazing ways. Parenting you is unquestionably one of the hardest things we have ever done, but in exchange you have taught us about the meaning and power of unconditional love. We are better humans because of you. Thank you for making our hearts grow and beat beyond ourselves.

To all of our extended family, and especially Ashley, Nate, Bodie, Stella, Deanna, and Rob, thank you for being a central part of our support system on a daily basis. Your presence in our lives always makes difficult days easier. We appreciate you more than you know.

To Alyssa Milano, thank you for improving our world with your encouraging social and political causes. Thank you for standing up for women's rights and igniting the worldwide #MeToo movement. Thank you for sharing our work with others. And thank you for writing the foreword to this book. We are forever grateful for your positive presence in our lives.

To our agent, Rick Richter, thank you for believing in us when we didn't believe in ourselves. Thank you for talking us through our initial hesitation to seek a publisher for the idea that led to this book. You absolutely pushed and pulled us through the self-doubts that would have prevented these very words from being written.

To Janna Marlies Maron and Matt Gartland, thank you for helping us map out and edit the rough draft of this book. Your insight and support, on this and previous projects, have been incredibly enlightening and have allowed us to shine. We sincerely look forward to working with you on future projects.

To our editor, Marian Lizzi, thank you for remixing our words, improving our punch lines, and directing us through the process of writing a far better book than we ever could have without your expert guidance. We sincerely appreciate the way you led us in the right direction without being pushy. You are a true professional who leads with a personal touch.

To our close friends Janet and Cami, and all the strong women and men we've worked with over the years, who have grown through incredible loss and adversity, thank you. There was a time when each of you came to us feeling stuck and lost, unaware of your own brilliance, and blind to the fact that your struggles had strengthened you and given you a resilient upper hand in this crazy world. But now you all are honestly our biggest heroes. Over the years you have collectively given us more than we could ever possibly give back. You continue to be our greatest source of inspiration on a daily basis. And you are the single greatest reason we wanted to write this book in the first place. We are forever indebted to you and your heart-centered journeys back to happy.